Introduction

Welcome to the second volume of J-Crowned, a series of books which seeks to preserve the memory and honour the legacy of the professional wrestlers contained within. Thank you very much for being here, wherever you are, to read this.

From Karl Gotch to Hiroshi Tanahashi, there is a long history of wrestlers being referred to as gods, in fact, pro-wrestling is perhaps the grandest polytheistic religion of our times. In Volume 1 of J-Crowned we looked at the men who had claimed arguably the greatest prizes in all of professional wrestling, people who are (in the main, at least) in no danger of being forgotten any time soon. Volume 2 broadens the range of subjects included, men and women who have all fought on the grandest of stages and who have all been transmuted by their mastery of the spectacle and the glory they achieved in the wrestling ring. However, as our roll-call of deities grows longer and our memories shorter, some of these gods are in danger of fading from our thoughts altogether.

Wrestlers are, of course, flesh and blood. All subjects included in this book have risked their lives by pursuing their profession, all have endured layers of physical and emotional suffering that are hard for the spectator to comprehend. The lucky make it through their careers unscathed, while some are hurt to the point where their lives are ruined and some, sadder still, are so damaged that they ruin the lives of others.

The biographies included in this book are intended to be neutral and this book is intended as a celebration of professional wrestling. It is my hope that reading of familiar names will bring a smile to the reader's face and that reading about an unknown grappler encourages further research on the part of the reader to further celebrate the subject. These men and women gave their lives to this, to us, and this book is a small step taken against the forgetting of such sacrifice. I can only hope you enjoy it.

IWGP JR. HEAVYWEIGHT CHAMPIONSHIP

Since 1973 the heavyweights of New Japan could battle over the NWF Heavyweight title and latterly, from 1983, fight for the annual trophy of the IWGP Championship belt awarded to the winner of the IWGP tournament. For the junior heavyweights the premier title of New Japan's early years was another that owed its name to a different promotion, that of the WWF Junior Heavyweight Championship.

Although never usurping Inoki at the top of the card, the junior bouts offered something different and led to figures such as Fujinami and Tiger Mask driving ticket sales in their own right. In addition to celebrating home grown stars, the Jr. Heavyweight Championship always had an international antagonist vying for its ownership, whether it was Rollerball Rocco as Black Tiger or The Dynamite Kid doing battle with local heroes, the division became a true highlight of NJPW in early nineteen eighties.

The wrestling landscape never stands still, however, and 1985 saw the WWF enter the Wrestlemania era, duly severing its working relationship with New Japan, reacquiring and promptly retiring the Jr. Heavyweight championship on 31st of October. Just four months later on February 6th, 1986, the final WWF Jr. Heavyweight champion, The Cobra, fought Shiro Koshinaka, a young man who had arrived in New Japan from All Japan via an excursion with EMLL in Mexico, for the honour of being crowned the first ever IWGP Jr. Heavyweight champion. Koshinaka won and the lineage of one of New Japan's most storied championships had its start, over a year before that of its heavyweight counterpart.

Although the IWGP Jr. Heavyweight championship has had mixed fortunes in terms of the focus the company has placed on it over the years, the performances of those men who have been drawn from all over the world to do battle for it have never been less than innovative and awe inspiring. The Junior division itself has reliably produced wrestlers who have gone on to top the card as heavyweights or as legends who transcend weight limits and the IWGP Jr. Heavyweight championship remains an unwavering symbol of their excellence.

1. Shiro Koshinaka

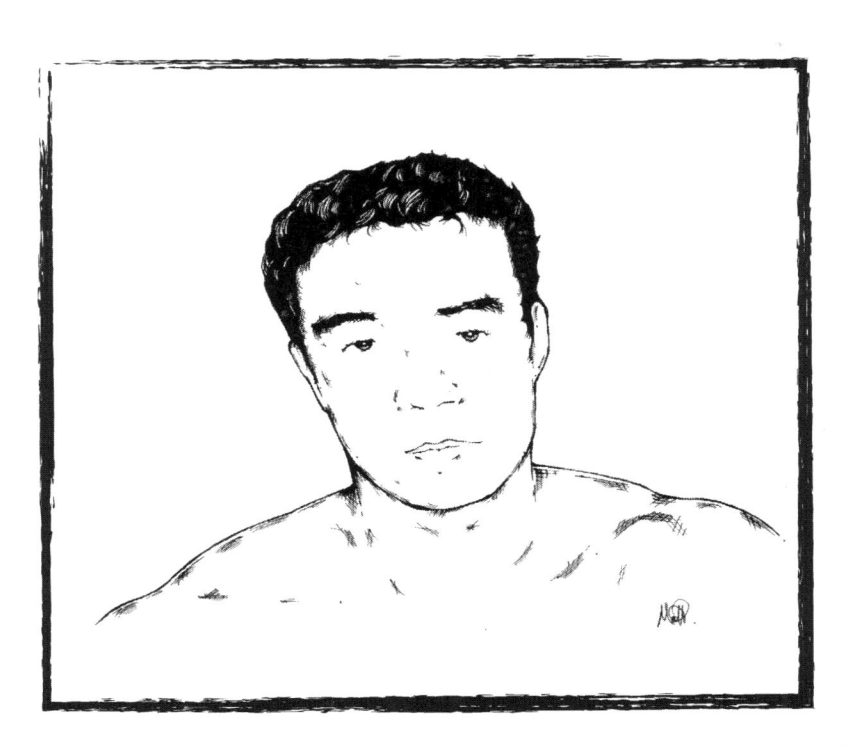

Shiro Koshinaka was a product of the AJPW dojo, trained by Giant Baba he debuted in 1979 and began a two year spell without a win, learning his craft through defeat. Gaining respect and momentum through sterling performances against touring figures such as Chavo Guerrero (from whom he learnt his famed hip attack) and Dos Caras, Koshinaka would frequently clash with Mitsuharu Misawa, defeating him in the finals of the 1983 Lou Thesz Cup and seemed to be on the brink of great things within Baba's All Japan. But it was not to be, sent on excursion to Mexico for the duration of 1984, Koshinaka could only watch from afar as Baba put the Tiger Mask on Misawa and Tiger Mask II captured the imagination of the viewing audience.

Returning from Mexico, Koshinaka landed directly in NJPW and found himself truly appreciated, spending his first year victorious or strongly protected in defeat. Momentum brought him to clash with The Cobra on the 6th of February 1986 and victory saw him become the first ever IWGP Jr. Heavyweight Champion. From that moment on there was no stauncher defender of New Japan honour in battles with the likes of Maeda, Takada and Fujiwara. Accumulating three Junior Heavyweight Championship reigns, Koshinaka was an impactful, much loved figure and stayed that way long after moving to the heavyweight division in 1990.

REIGNS
1. 06/02/1986 (DEFEATED: The Cobra) - 19/04/1986 (LOST TO: Nobuhiko Takada)
2. 19/09/1986 (DEFEATED: Nobuhiko Takada) - 02/08/1987 (LOST TO: vacated due to injury)
3. 24/06/1988 (DEFEATED: Owen Hart)- 16/03/1989 (LOST TO: Hiroshi Hase)
• Combined days as champion: 702
• Combined defences: 9

2. Nobuhiko Takada

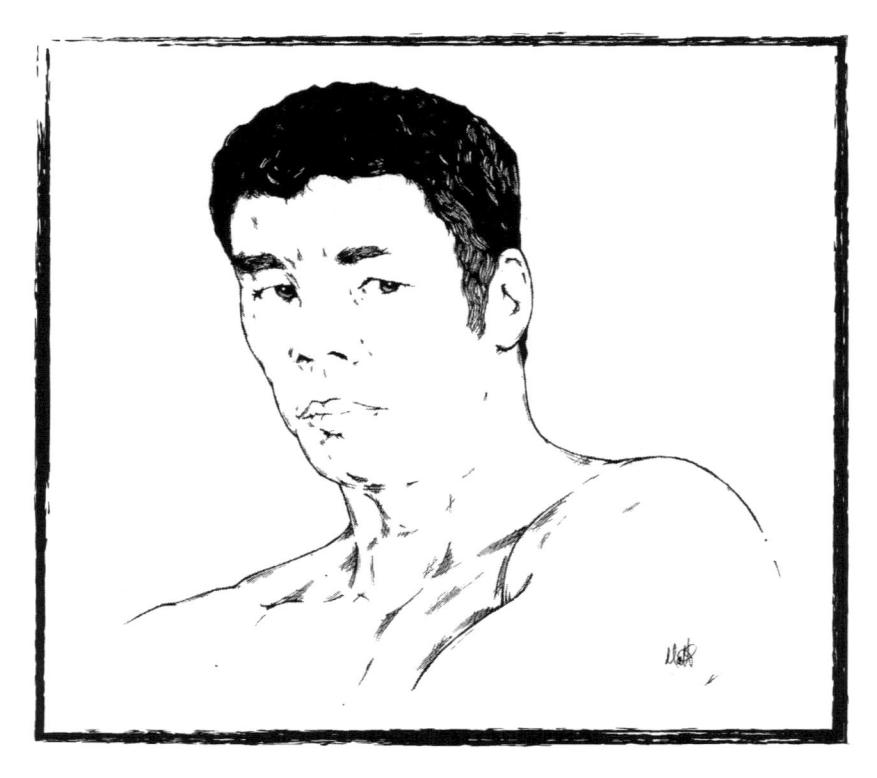

Takada came through the New Japan dojo, primarily trained by Yoshiaki Fujiwara. Showing great aptitude in his early years and impressing to such an extent that he was appointed assistant to Antonio Inoki, success looked sure to come for Takada in the WWF Jr. Heavyweight division.

However, in 1984, Fujiwara, Takada and Tiger Mask (Satoru Sayama) left NJPW to join the fledgling, shoot-style, UWF. UWF blazed an inspirational trail, but soon burnt out, and the majority of wrestlers that had left NJPW in 1984 returned under the guise of invaders in 1986.

In May, Takada began to torture Shiro Koshinaka in tag matches, eventually leading to an IWGP Jr. Heavyweight Title match on the 19th of that month which Takada won. Holding the title over the summer of 1986, Takada defended it against the best of the Junior division in very short order, 6 defences in just four months, before losing it back to Koshinaka in September.

1987 would see Akira Maeda teamed with Takada to reap havoc in the tag division, before the forming of a new UWF saw them depart from New Japan once more. Takada would return a heavyweight to invade one more time in 1995, changing the whole world in the process.

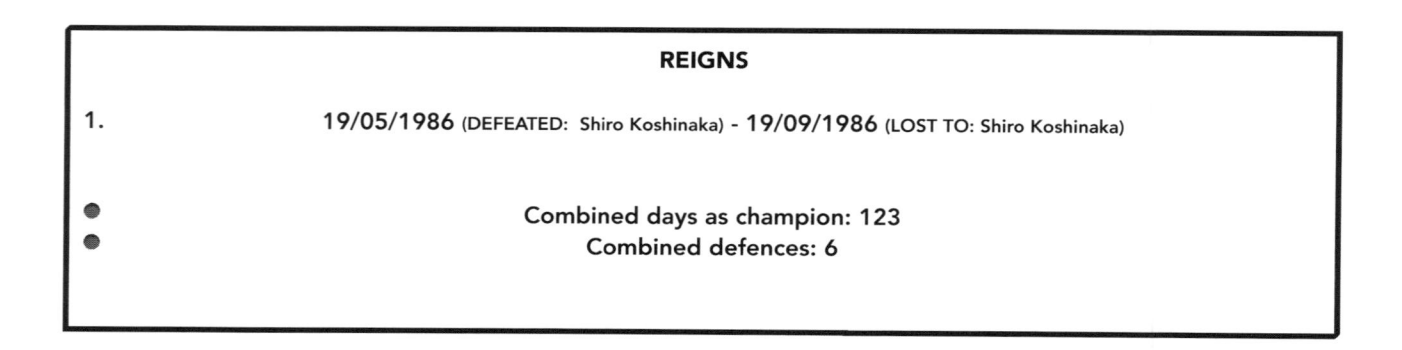

REIGNS
1. 19/05/1986 (DEFEATED: Shiro Koshinaka) - 19/09/1986 (LOST TO: Shiro Koshinaka)
Combined days as champion: 123
Combined defences: 6

3. Kuniaki Kobayashi

Kobayashi began his career in NJPW, debuting in the company's very early days, starting out in 1973 when he was just 17. Growing up battling some of the great juniors of the era, Kobayashi´s fundamentals were all in place, but a two year spell in Mexico with EMLL and the UWA alongside appearances for NWA Hollywood, put the finishing touches on the athlete and he returned to NJPW in 1982 a swaggering villain, quicker and smoother in the ring than before.

He returned for the October tour, wrestled 16 matches in 22 days, culminating in his challenging for the WWF Jr. Heavyweight Championship then held by Tiger Mask, the first of several classics he would have with Sayama and the Dynamite Kid.

Kobayashi departed New Japan with Choshu and the rest of Ishin Gundan in 1984 and spent the following three years in AJPW, where he became the second World Jr. Heavyweight champion in company history and also won the storied NWA International Jr. Heavyweight Title.

So it was as a widely respected international veteran at the peak of his powers, that Kobayashi returned to NJPW in May 1987. Koshinaka had vacated his title due to injury and there was a two night tournament in which the fan favourite Kobayashi defeated Masakatsu Funaki, Tatsutoshi Goto and Nobuhiko Takada to finally be crowned the IWGP Jr. Heavyweight Champion. He would soon lose the belt to Hase and only challenge for it twice more, before moving up to the Heavyweight division in 1990. Kobayashi is warmly regarded, yet not discussed as frequently as he should be, as a true great amidst a golden age of junior heavyweight talent.

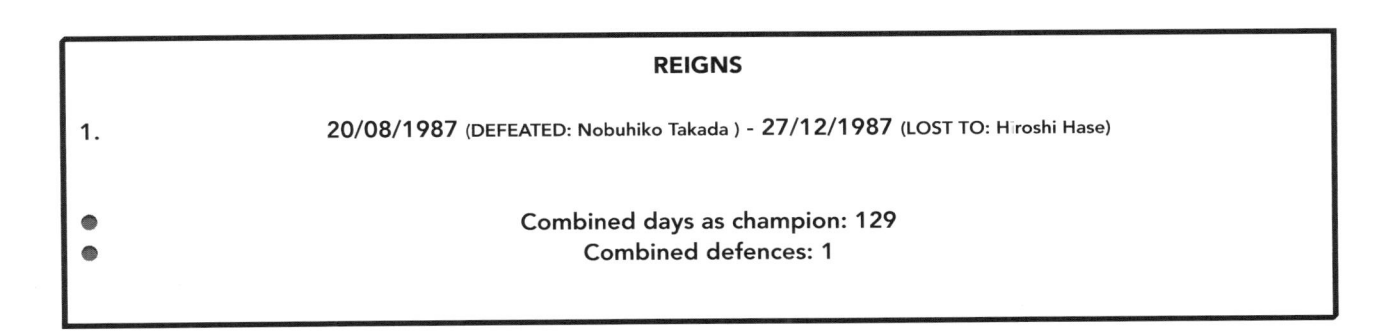

REIGNS
1.   20/08/1987 (DEFEATED: Nobuhiko Takada) - 27/12/1987 (LOST TO: Hiroshi Hase)
Combined days as champion: 129 Combined defences: 1

4. Hiroshi Hase

An accomplished amateur wrestler, who had represented Japan in the 1984 Olympics, Hase transitioned to pro-wrestling under the tutelage of Riki Choshu. To complete his training, Hase was sent to work for Stampede Wrestling under the legendary technician Stu Hart, were he would spend a year and a half wrestling with the best the territory had to offer including long programs with Brian Pillman and Owen Hart.

Leaving Canada a refined pro-wrestling machine, Hase signed with New Japan and proceeded to win the IWGP Jr. Heavyweight Championship on his debut in an outstanding match at the year end show, 1987.

An immediate star, Hase reached the finals of the first ever Top of the Super Juniors Tournament holding his title until it was Owen Hart´s turn to visit New Japan on a learning excursion of his own. Hase would stay in contention for the Jr. Heavyweight championship, holding it once more in 1989 before moving to the Heavyweight division with the advent of the new decade.

REIGNS
1.   27/12/1987 (DEFEATED: Kuniaki Kobayashi) - 27/05/1988 (LOST TO: Owen Hart)
2.   16/03/1989 (DEFEATED: Shiro Koshinaka) - 25/05/1989 (LOST TO: Jushin Liger)
• Combined days as champion: 195
• Combined defences: 3

5. Owen Hart

Youngest son of Stu Hart, Owen was trained in the famous family dungeon and started working for his father's Stampede Wrestling at the age of 18 in 1983. Having great chemistry with young NJPW stars like Keiichi Yamada (Liger) and Hiroshi Hase as they passed through the territory, New Japan was Owen's first overseas destination when looking to develop his abilities further.

A tour in summer 1987 saw him challenge Kuniaki Kobayashi for the IWGP Jr. Heavyweight Championship for the first time and this encounter was followed by an eye opening performance in the first ever Top of the Super Juniors tournament in which he finished fourth.

On his next tour he faced an old friend and rival, Hiroshi Hase, on 27th of May 1988. Following a grappling classic, Owen emerged victorious, capturing the IWGP Jr. Heavyweight Championship and, with his victory, became the first non-Japanese wrestler to do so. Koshinaka reclaimed the title for New Japan on the penultimate day of Hart's tour, with Owen going on to spend a year with the WWF. A few more tours with New Japan would be in Owen's future and his time spent with the company contributed greatly to the reputation and development of the future legend.

REIGNS

1. 27/05/1998 (DEFEATED: Hiroshi Hase) - 24/06/1998 (LOST TO: Shiro Koshinaka)

- Combined days as champion: 28
- Combined defences: 1

6. Jushin Thunder Liger

Keiichi Yamada came through the same New Japan dojo class as Muto, Chono and Hashimoto, having gone through rejection and adversity before even getting his feet in the door. Athletic and powerful, an accomplished amateur wrestler, Yamada showed great promise; winning as many matches as he lost in his debut year of 1984, reaching the finals of the first Young Lion´s cup in 1985 and challenging for the IWGP Junior Heavyweight championship for the first time in July 1986 before leaving for his international learning excursion. Time spent abroad with Stampede in Canada and All Star Promotions in England fully prepared Yamada to set the world alight when he returned to New Japan; however, despite his excellent athletic base and spectacular moves he found himself floundering in his connection with the crowd. In early 1989 he returned to Europe in an attempt to find himself, yet something all-together different found him.

After first offering the role to his travelling partner Masakatsu Funaki, the New Japan office turned to Yamada to portray the masked protagonist of a new manga and Saturday afternoon cartoon, Jushin Liger, which NJPW had licensed in order to stay relevant with younger viewers. Debuting on the first ever pro-wrestling show in the Tokyo Dome, Liger was quick, colourful, strong and victorious, defeating the veteran Kuniaki Kobayashi with a German Suplex, so beginning the most extraordinary decade of dominance and global scale success. Visually unlike anyone else, with a body suit which evolved along with the Beast God of the anime (which came to an end in 1990), physically capable of great athleticism and pure power, innovative and possessing of a humility which made him a hugely popular and trusted opponent and standard bearer for NJPW.

Earning his first run with the IWGP Junior title in May 1989 with a win over Hiroshi Hase, Liger was the NJPW figurehead for the 90s Junior division. Making household names of his rivals The Great Sasuke, El Samurai and Último Dragón both in Japan and, via his appearances on WCW TV, in the States. Surviving a brain tumour and adapting his wrestling style to one which was more sustainable, in total, Liger had 11 reigns as IWGP Junior Heavyweight Champion, spending over six year as champion across those reigns. Any summary of his greatness and lasting significance within pro wrestling is destined to fall short, but simply put, there is no greater unifying figure in all of wrestling than the legendary Jushin Thunder Liger.

REIGNS

1. 25/05/1989 (DEFEATED: Hiroshi Hase) - 10/08/1989 (LOST TO: Naoki Sano)
2. 31/01/1990 (DEFEATED: Naoki Sano) - 19/08/1990 (LOST TO: Pegasus Kid)
3. 01/11/1990 (DEFEATED: Pegasus Kid) - 15/04/1991 (Vacated to be defended in Top of Super Juniors)
4. 12/06/1991 (DEFEATED: Norio Honaga) - 09/08/1991 (LOST TO: Akira Nogami)
5. 08/02/1992 (DEFEATED: Norio Honaga) - 26/06/1992 (LOST TO: El Samurai)
6. 04/01/1993 (DEFEATED: Último Dragón) - 24/09/1994 (Vacated due to injury)
7. 04/01/1996 (DEFEATED: Koji Kanemoto) - 29/14/1996 (LOST TO: The Great Sasuke)
8. 04/01/1997 (DEFEATED: Último Dragón) - 06/07/1997 (LOST TO: El Samurai)
9. 07/02/1998 (DEFEATED: Shinjiro Otani) - 17/03/1999 (LOST TO: Koji Kanemoto)
10. 11/10/1999 (DEFEATED: Kendo Kashin) - 29//11/1999 (LOST TO: Juventud Guerrera)
11. 06/12/1999 (DEFEATED: Juventud Guerrera) - 20/07/2000 (LOST TO: Tatsuhito Takaiwa)

- Combined days as champion: : 2245
- Combined defences: 31

7.Naoki Sano

Naoki Sano graduated from the New Japan dojo on March 3rd 1984 and spent the first three years of his career trading victories in opening bouts with his contemporaries : Hashimoto, Muto, Chono and, most notably, Keiichi Yamada who debuted on exactly the same day as Sano. In 1987 Sano was sent on a learning excursion to Mexico where he added greater flair to his already proficient technical base and captured his first championship, the Distrito Federal Trios title, alongside Hirokazu Hata and the future Ultimo Dragon, Yoshihiro Asai.

Sano returned to Japan in January 1989 just as NJPW were building toward their first wrestling show in the newly opened Tokyo Dome. The opening match on the first Tokyo Dome card was the final of the 1989 Young Lion Cup, which Sano had advanced to via victories over Iizuka and Honaga. He was the first wrestler to walk to the ring in the Dome and also the first to have his hand raised in victory as he beat Hiro Saito to win the tournament. On the same night, Keiichi Yamada made his first appearance under a mask as Jushin Liger.

Liger rocketed to the top of the Junior Heavyweight division and Naoki Sano became his first true rival. They first met in battle on July 13th 1989, with the match ending in a double knock out, this led to a rematch one month later which saw Sano defeat Liger to win the IWGP Junior Heavyweight Championship. Liger challenged the following month, but Sano retained, as he also did when he met Owen Hart in defense of his title on the same tour. However, on the 31st of January 1990, an evolved Jushin Thunder Liger returned to defeat Sano and bring his one championship reign to an end.

Shortly after, Sano was tempted away from NJPW by a contract with the short-lived SWS promotion and he would then join UWF-I and Battlarts, excelling as a serious technical grappler. He found great success in Pro-Wrestling NOAH, but Sano's career remained tied to New Japan and twinned with Liger's. Sano returned to battle and then team with Liger in the Tokyo Dome in January 2020 in what would be the final two matches of both men's careers.

REIGNS
1.   10/08/1989 (DEFEATED: Jushin Liger) - 31/01/1990 (LOST TO: Jushin Thunder Liger)
Combined days as champion: 174
Combined defences: 2

8. Pegasus Kid

Initially trained by Stu Hart, Chris Benoit debuted for Stampede Wrestling in late 1985 where he modelled himself after greats who had passed through that promotion, The Dynamite Kid and Bret Hart.

Intense and eye catching, Benoit first appeared in NJPW in 1986, spending much of the following year on excursion with the company and furthering his training in the dojo. Returning to Stampede, Benoit spent the subsequent years as a heavily decorated champion, until the company closed its doors for good at the end of 1989.

Donning a mask and the new name Pegasus Kid, Benoit moved out to Japan to begin a full-time program with NJPW; finding instant success, he went undefeated until challenging Liger in March 1990 for the IWGP Jr. Heavyweight Championship. A match which he lost, but in which he demonstrated his growth and abilities to an appreciative audience which ensured he would stay in contention for the title that he would finally capture in August of the same year. His reign was short, losing it back to Liger in November, but Benoit stayed at the top in Japan, feuding and partnering with the very best of the international and local junior heavyweights as his career an renown exploded on a global level in the early 90s, finally seeing him leave Japan for WCW on a permanent basis in 1995.

REIGNS
1. 19/08/1990 (DEFEATED: Jushin Thunder Liger) - 01/11/1990 (LOST TO: Jushin Thunder Liger)
Combined days as champion: 74
Combined defences: 1

9. Norio Honaga

Debuting for New Japan in April 1980, Honaga´s early career path followed the map laid out for the majority of young lions, two years on the under card learning the ropes before an excursion abroad to broaden their knowledge base.

It was on returning from Mexico in 1984 that things took a turn for the different for Honaga, leaving NJPW with the exodus led by Choshu, Honaga found himself in the blossoming mid-80s environment of All Japan. During his time in AJPW Honaga grew considerably as a performer, becoming a tag-team champion along the way, so when he returned to NJPW alongside a lot of his cohorts in 1987 it was as a well respected all-rounder.

Despite this, it would be through tournaments that Honaga primarily challenged for the IWGP Jr. Heavyweight Championship, unsuccessfully in August 1987, but then triumphantly winning the title alongside the Top of the Super Juniors in 1991. His victory put him into more regular title contention, yet he would fall short each time he faced Liger, fittingly his last IWGP Championship run came as he won the tournament necessitated by Liger vacating the title in 1994. His final run being his strongest, five successful defences against varied opponents and styles, he would retire four years later a greatly respected career junior heavyweight.

	REIGNS
1.	30/04/1991 (DEFEATED: Jushin Thunder Liger) - 12/06/1991 (LOST TO: Jushin Thunder Liger)
2.	05/11/1991 (DEFEATED: Akira Nogami) - 08/02/1992 (LOST TO: Jushin Thunder Liger)
3.	27/09/1994 (DEFEATED: Wild Pegasus)- 19/02/1995 (LOST TO: Koji Kanemoto)

- Combined days as champion: 283
- Combined defences: 9

10. Akira Nogami

Nogami graduated from the New Japan Dojo at the age of 18 in 1984. He was a crisp technician, forged by his experiences with his notable contemporaries, his first three matches in New Japan were losing efforts against Muto, Chono and Hashimoto and the following few years working alongside such luminaries shaped a highly competent grappler.

The years that followed saw Nogami as something of a place holder in the junior division, gaining wins over debuting talent and helping them find their feet in the ring, yet never challenging for top honours in his own right.

This changed in 1990, the face of the division having been transformed by the explosive popularity of the spectacular Liger, Akira Nogami returned from an excursion in Europe as the Kabuki styled AKIRA, replete with colourful entrance attire and painted face. In this form he unsuccessfully challenged Liger in the Tokyo Dome at Starrcade 1991, forcing a rematch in August of the same year. Nogami employed the resilience developed over the duration of his career to weather the storm of Liger's offence and prevail with pure wrestling ability, scoring a deserved win with a bridging Butterfly Suplex. Three months later and the title would be lost to Honaga and AKIRA would move up to the Heavyweight division having carved his name into history with his triumph over Liger.

REIGNS

1. **09/08/1991** (DEFEATED: Jushin Thunder Liger) - **05/11/1991** (LOST TO: Norio Honaga)

- Combined days as champion: 88
- Combined defences: 1

11. El Samurai

Joining the NJPW dojo on completing high school, Osamu Matsuda debuted under his own name for the company in July 1986. He would spend nearly five years wrestling with his peers and touring newcomers until departing for Mexico on his learning excursion in 1991, where, on arrival he was given a mask and rechristened El Samurai.

His stay lasted a year and his return was somewhat notable, re-emerging on New Japan's 20th anniversary show to defeat the Kanemoto iteration of Tiger Mask, El Samurai was destined to be a contender. Combining power moves with crisp submission work, he reached the finals of the 1992 Top of the Super Juniors, earning two matches for the IWGP Jr. Heavyweight title with Liger, gaining victory at his second attempt. This first reign yielded career defining defences against Benoit, Malenko and Liger himself before being brought to an end by the debuting Último Dragón.

In 1997 a reinvigorated El Samurai won the Best of the Super Juniors and earned the right to face Liger once more. At this time, the two were teaming in a feud in which they were battling against the emerging generation of juniors, Samurai was victorious over Liger, but quickly lost to the leader of this new generation, Shinjiro Otani. Unsuccessful in any future attempt to claim the IWGP Jr. Heavyweight championship, El Samurai transitioned to the role of gatekeeper, a vital veteran, eventually leaving NJPW in 2007.

REIGNS

1. **26/06/1992** (DEFEATED: Jushin Thunder Liger) - **22/11/1992** (LOST TO: Último Dragón)
2. **06/07/1997** (DEFEATED: Jushin Thunder Liger) - **10/08/1997** (LOST TO: Shinjiro Otani)

- Combined days as champion: 184
- Combined defences: 3

12. Último Dragón

Yoshihiro Asai was a product of the NJPW dojo who graduated in 1987 but left the company shortly after his debut, failing to find his feet in what can be the dispiriting grind of a young lion's life. He moved to Mexico to further his training under legendary Japanese luchador Gran Hamada, finding instant success with UWA, UWF and EMLL.

Asai returned to Japan to work a number of shows for the short lived melting pot of a promotion SWS, before retuning to CMLL where he adopted the mask and name of Último Dragón (The Last Dragon). As SWS dissolved, CMLL established a working relationship with Tenryu's WAR who, in turn, produced a number of shows feuding with New Japan. It was in this capacity that the young man who had once left NJPW, returned a transformed prospect, a completely unique hybrid warrior on 22nd November 1992 to beat El Samurai for the IWGP Jr. Heavyweight Title.

His reign was ended in spectacular fashion in a thrilling contest with Liger at the Tokyo Dome in 1993. The pattern would repeat three years later, balancing his time between Mexico, Japan and the USA, primarily a WAR talent, Dragón defeated The Great Sasuke on a WAR show in Osaka in October to win the IWGP Jr. Heavyweight Championship as part of the J-Crown. In just two months, he defended the title seven times in both the States and Japan before Liger reclaimed the belt at the Tokyo Dome. During this time Dragón built a legacy for himself that endures to this very day, a peerless innovator, popularising spectacular high-flying combined with supreme submission skills.

REIGNS

1. 22/11/1992 (DEFEATED: El Samurai) - 04/01/1993 (LOST TO: Jushin Thunder Liger)
2. 11/10/1996 (DEFEATED: The Great Sasuke) - 04/01/1997 (LOST TO: Jushin Thunder Liger)

- Combined days as champion: 128
- Combined defences: 8

13. Koji Kanemoto

A championship winning judoka, Kanemoto was scouted by New Japan, enrolling in the NJPW dojo and debuting in late 1990. Lightening quick, incorporating vicious kicks alongside proficient mat technique, he showed great promise and was awarded the Tiger Mask gimmick following a tour of Mexico in 1993. His first match under the Tiger Mask name was a victory over Liger, yet in this guise he never went after the Junior Heavyweight Championship, ultimately losing a classic mask vs mask contest with Liger at the 1994 January Dome show before returning to Mexico for most of the year.

1995 would be the first real year of Kanemoto dominance. Returning under his own name at the Tokyo Dome he put the world on notice with a grappling clinic and victory against Nagata, capturing the Jr. Heavyweight Championship a month later. He shone in the NJPW feud against the UWF and defeated all challengers; with the exception of a month in the company of Sabu, the Jr. Heavyweight championship was his for a year until he came up against Liger once more in the Tokyo Dome.

In essence, this is Kanemoto´s story, a dominant compelling technician deeply admired, yet capable of being loathsome when required, overshadowed in memory by the larger than life figures who he helped to shine all the brighter. Kanemoto´s lengthy career at the top of his game allowed him to tend the flame of the division and pass the torch with two further excellent reigns in the new millennium.

REIGNS

1. 19/02/1995 (DEFEATED: Norio Honaga) - 03/05/1995 (LOST TO: Sabu)
2. 14/06/1995 (DEFEATED: Sabu) - 04/01/1996 (LOST TO: Jushin Thunder Liger)
3. 17/03/1997 (DEFEATED: Jushin Thunder Liger) - 28/08/1997 (LOST TO: Kendo Kashin)
4. 19/07/2002 (DEFEATED: Minoru Tanaka) - 23/04/2003 (LOST TO: Tiger Mask IV)
5. 03/05/2006 (DEFEATED: Tiger Mask IV) - 24/12/2006 (LOST TO: Minoru Tanaka)

Combined days as champion: 954
Combined defences: 14

14. Sabu

Trained by and modelling himself after his uncle, the legendary, bloodthirsty, Sheik, Sabu first appeared in Japan in late 1991 teaming with his uncle for FMW. Wrestling almost exclusively for FMW for the following three years, Sabu's style pushed all boundaries of reason, especially for the time, combining high flying risk taking with a penchant for barbed wire, tables, fire and explosives.

His fame increased throughout 1994, but, while he began to accept more bookings in the United States, Japan was still where Sabu's career lay and on Christmas Eve 1994 he debuted for NJPW.

In May 1995 he clashed with Koji Kanemoto to become IWJP Jr. Heavyweight Champion. He defended the title once against the Eddie Guerrero incarnation of Black Tiger on the twelfth of June, before losing it back to Kanemoto two days later. Sabu spent the rest of the year mostly with New Japan, an attraction and a genuine highlight reel wherever he went, though even greater fame awaited him as an ECW icon.

REIGNS

1. 03/05/1995 (DEFEATED: Koji Kanemoto) - 14/06/1995 (LOST TO: Koji Kanemoto)

- Combined days as champion: 42
- Combined defences: 1

15. The Great Sasuke

In 1990 Masanori Murakawa failed in his attempt to enter the New Japan Dojo and almost walked away from wrestling entirely. Thankfully, his path instead took him to the UWF where he worked under the name Masa Michinoku, and then for much of 1992 to Mexico where he developed a hybrid lucha/martial art style of grappling and changed his name to Ninja Sasuke.

Returning to Japan in 1993 he changed his name one more time to the Great Sasuke and adopted his iconic Kabuki inspired mask. Breaking away from the UWF with a huge swathe of fellow talent, Sasuke founded Michinoku Pro, the first Japanese independent promotion not based in or in the immediate vicinity of Tokyo.

Developing a reputation as a hotbed of cutting edge new talent, Michinoku Pro played a huge part in NJPW´s legendary 1994 Super J-Cup Tournament; with Sasuke, Taka Michinoku and Super Delfin all participating, Sasuke made it to the final only to lose to Wild Pegasus. Forming a relationship of great trust with New Japan and Jushin Thunder Liger immediately through his breathtaking performance on the show, Sasuke became a huge star overnight.

Through 1994/5 Sasuke continued to augment his reputation, accumulating junior heavyweight titles in a number of promotions, culminating with a return to NJPW in April 1996 and a match at the Tokyo Dome in which he toppled Liger to win the IWGP Jr. Heavyweight Championship. Liger subsequently went to Michinoku Pro and won their Jr. Heavyweight title and the seeds for the J-Crown were planted. Over a four-night tournament, eight junior heavyweight champions from all over the world clashed in August 1996 with all of their titles on the line. The Great Sasuke again stole the show and truly stood on top of the world on the fifth of August as the first ever J-Crown Champion. He would be relieved of the weight of all of that gold just two months later by the man he had defeated in the final, Último Dragón, but Sasuke´s exploits at this time and his remarkable durability alongside his independent genius have set him apart as a legend for the ages.

REIGNS

1. 23/04/1996 (DEFEATED: Jushin Thunder Liger) - 11/10/1996 (LOST TO: Último Dragón)

-
-

Combined days as champion: 165
Combined defences: 5

CLASSIC MATCH N°1

Date: 29th April 1996
Location: Tokyo Dome, Tokyo
Attendance: 65,000

THE GREAT SASUKE vs JUSHIN THUNDER LIGER

Star-crossed rivals raising the bar for all who follow. A packed Tokyo Dome saw Sasuke capture the IWGP Jr. Heavyweight Championship from his nemesis Liger in an all time classic.

16. Shinjiro Otani

Graduating from the NJPW dojo at the age of 19, Otani debuted for New Japan in the summer of 1992. A gifted mat wrestler who would incorporate spring-board attacks effectively, Otani shone in his early matches with and against his dojo contemporary Yuji Nagata and would benefit greatly from participating in major tournaments throughout ´93 and ´94.

Another pairing that would greatly benefit the young Otani was with Wild Pegasus (Chris Benoit) with the two winning the Super Grade Jr. Heavyweight Tag League together in 1994, establishing Otani as a true contender in double quick time. The final of the 1995 Best of the Super Juniors was contested between these two, a match which Pegasus would win, only for Otani to gain a significant measure of revenge and a huge boost to his global name value when he defeated Pegasus to become the inaugural WCW Cruiserweight Champion in spring 1996.

After another year of contendership and holding secondary junior accolades, 1997 was finally Otani´s year to capture the IWGP Jr. Heavyweight Championship, defeating El Samurai in order to claim it as part of the J-Crown. Vacating all titles other than the IWGP Jr. Heavyweight Championship, following the WWF once more demanding the return of one of their titles, Otani was a strong defending champion, surviving the New Year's Dome Show and the challenge of Último Dragón before falling to the inevitable Liger in early 1998.

Despite further success in the division´s tag-ranks, New Japan began a phase of de-emphasising the importance of the junior heavyweights in 2000/2001, pushing Otani to battle as a heavyweight; in which time he would notably challenge Sasaki for the IWGP Heavyweight Championship. A disillusioned Otani joined Zero-One at its inception and has remained one of its cornerstones ever since.

REIGNS
1.   10/08/1997 (DEFEATED: El Samurai) - 07/02/1998 (LOST TO: Jushin Thunder Liger)
• • Combined days as champion: 181 Combined defences: 5

17. Kendo Kashin

Debuting for New Japan in 1992 under his own name, Tokimitsu Ishizawa, his first few years saw the future Kashin struggling to gain traction as a mostly mat based submission wrestler amidst more spectacular contemporaries.

However, 1995 and a feud with UWF-I brought Ishizawa more into the limelight as he represented NJPW in its war with the shooters. Early 1996 saw him win the Young Lion's Cup before heading to Germany for the second half of the year on his learning excursion and it was here that he donned the mask and adopted the new name Kendo Kashin.

He returned in 1997 and spent the next two years in a more prominent role, winning the Junior Tag Titles with Dr. Wagner Jr., before winning the 1999 Best of the Super Juniors. The latter victory earning him the right to challenge Koji Kanemoto and claim the IWGP Jr. Heavyweight Championship for the first time, though the successful year would end on a flat note as he would lose the title swiftly to Liger.

The new millennium saw Kashin make forays into MMA, as New Japan under Inoki at this time wished to present the most legitimate fighters possible. Consequently, on gaining a somewhat fortunate victory over Ryan Gracie in July 2001, Kashin was granted an almost immediate IWGP title opportunity, which he seized to win the Junior Heavyweight Championship for the second time. A dominant championship reign ensued until Kashin jumped to rival promotion AJPW, voluntarily vacating his championship to continue his story elsewhere.

REIGNS

1. 28/08/1999 (DEFEATED: Koji Kanemoto) - 11/10/1999 (LOST TO: Jushin Thunder Liger)
2. 08/10/2001 (DEFEATED: Masayuki Naruse) - 01/02/2002 (LOST TO: Vacated on leaving the company)

- Combined days as champion: 160
- Combined defences: 3

18. Juventud Guerrera

Son of legendary luchador Fuerza Guerrera, Juventud began his career with AAA in 1992 and made his name primarily via an extended feud with his contemporary Rey Misterio Jr. In the mid-nineties the two wrestled a pair of ground breaking matches for ECW, putting Juventud on the international radar and leading to his first matches in Japan, with WAR in July 1996, again stealing the show with Rey Misterio.

Alongside many other luchadores of the era, Juventud was signed by WCW to help form the spectacular back bone of their cruiserweight division and it was through WCW´s working relationship with NJPW that Guerrera would challenge for the IWGP Jr. Heavyweight Championship. On a November 1999 episode of Nitro, Juventud defeated Liger via an underhand tequila bottle smash to become champion, but would tragically fracture his forearm in the week that followed leaving him unable to defend his newly won title. Psicosis would stand in for him and Liger reclaimed the championship on the following week´s episode of Nitro.

As the wrestling landscape changed with the new millennium, Juventud would return to Japan to compete primarily for NOAH in the 2000s.

REIGNS

1. **29/11/1999** (DEFEATED: Jushin Thunder Liger) - **06/12/1999** (LOST TO: Jushin Thunder Liger whilst substituted by Psicosis)

-
-

Combined days as champion: 7
Combined defences: 0

19. Tatsuhito Takaiwa

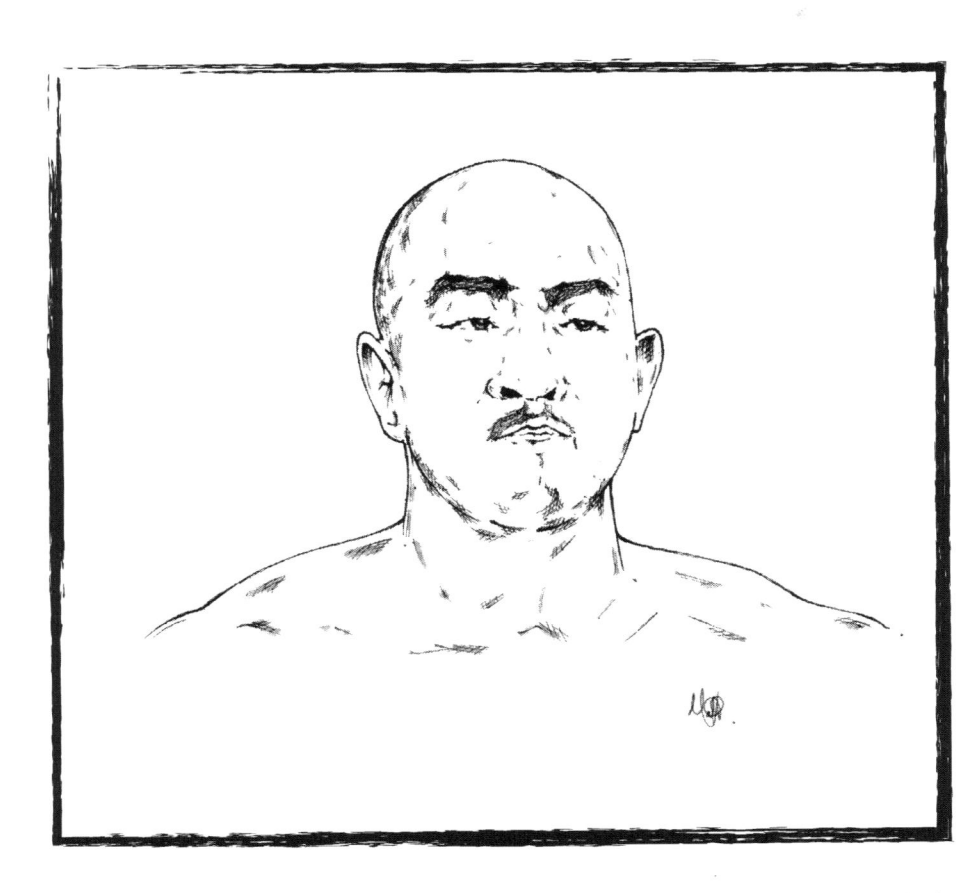

Debuting in the summer of 1992, Takaiwa was, for the longest time, the whipping boy of his dojo graduating class. The powerful young grappler would not truly begin to build momentum until 1996 when he begun to tag on more regular basis with his classmate Shinjiro Otani; a relationship which would see him challenge Otani for the J-Crown in September 1997. Unsuccessful in his challenge, but with a stronger partnership formed by competition, Takaiwa would win the IWGP Jr. Heavyweight Tag Team Titles alongside Otani in 1998 and their lengthy title reign established Takaiwa as a highly credible contender for singles honours.

Subsequently, Takaiwa unsuccessfully challenged Liger, Kanemoto and Kashin before, almost exactly eight years after his debut, he overcame Liger on 20th July 2000 to become IWGP Jr. Heavyweight Champion. A short reign ensued with defences over Kashin and Kanemoto before losing the title to the new sensation Minoru Tanaka in October.

At the turn of the new millennium Takaiwa left New Japan to experience enduring success with ZERO-1 and NOAH.

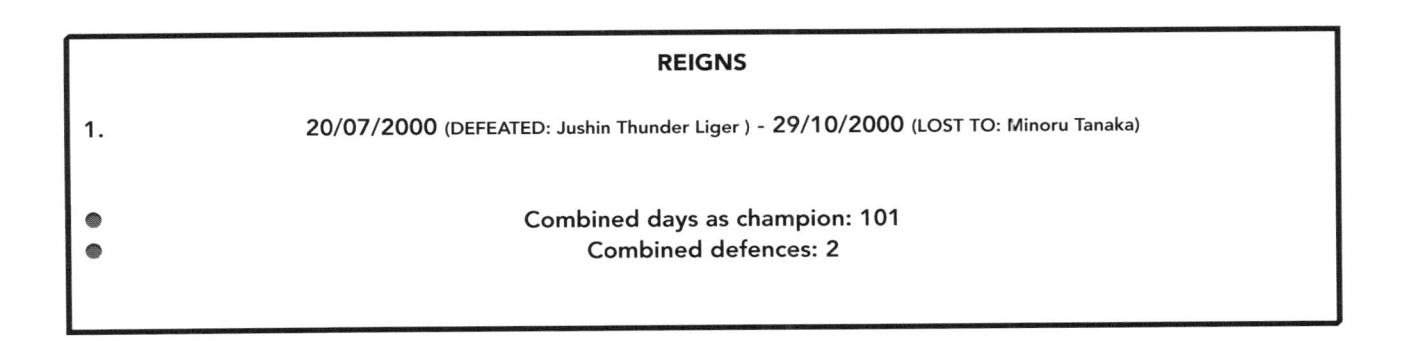

REIGNS
1. 20/07/2000 (DEFEATED: Jushin Thunder Liger) - 29/10/2000 (LOST TO: Minoru Tanaka)
Combined days as champion: 101
Combined defences: 2

20. Minoru Tanaka

Trained for pro-wrestling by Yoshiaki Fujiwara, Tanaka made his debut in 1994. Coming from a grappling and kickboxing background as a shoot-boxer, Tanaka showed immediate promise in his early years with Pro-Wrestling Fujiwara Gumi and Battlarts, becoming recognised as a leading light of junior heavyweight wrestling before his NJPW debut in 1999.

As a guest competitor in the 1999 Best of the Super Juniors Tournament Minoru Tanka instantly made a name for himself in the company, earning the right to challenge Kanemoto for the IWGP Jr. Heavyweight Championship in June 1999. Though unsuccessful in his challenge, his performance won him many new fans and sporadic guest appearances followed, generally challenging for the IWGP Jr. Singles or Tag Titles as he went back and forth between NJPW and Battlarts.

In June 2000, he won the tag titles alongside Kanemoto, in October he won the singles title from Takaiwa, in the process becoming a double champion and finally committing himself full time to New Japan. He would remain champion until July 2001 and stay in constant contention during his time with the company, winning the Junior Tag Titles five times and multiple tournaments including the 2006 Best of the Super Juniors, in addition to his total four reigns as Junior Heavyweight Champion.

All of his reigns were lengthy, 2004 was entirely his, whether wrestling under his full name, simply Minoru or under a mask as Heat, Minoru Tanaka was always at the centre of the division. Until time took its natural course and a new generation came up; 2008 saw Tanaka marginalised, resulting in his 2009 departure to AJPW where he experienced further extensive success.

REIGNS

1. 29/10/2000 (DEFEATED: Tatsuhito Takaiwa) - 20/07/2001 (LOST TO: Masayuki Naruse)
2. 16/02/2002 (DEFEATED: Masahito Kakihara) - 19/07/2002 (LOST TO: Koji Kanemoto)
3. 14/12/2003 (DEFEATED: Jado) - 04/01/2005 (LOST TO: Tiger Mask IV)
4. 24/12/2006 (DEFEATED: Koji Kanemoto) - 06/07/2007 (LOST TO: Ryusuke Taguchi)

- Combined days as champion: 998
- Combined defences: 20

21. Masayuki Naruse

Trained by the great Akira Maeda, Naruse debuted for the then pro-wrestling company Fighting Network Rings in 1992, before the company and its contracted talent transitioned to presenting MMA bouts in 1995. A talented grappler, Naruse accrued 9 wins and became the company's first Light Heavyweight Champion.

In 2001, during a period of uncertainty for RINGS, Naruse made the shrewd move of moving to New Japan which was in the midst of emphasising wrestlers with MMA backgrounds and whose reigning IWGP Jr. Heavyweight Champion was Minoru Tanaka, who had made his name as a star of Battlarts, RINGS' main competitor and rival. Positioned immediately as a direct challenge to Tanaka, Naruse triumphed on his in-ring debut for NJPW to win the Junior Heavyweight Championship on 20th of July 2001. His reign was short and ended in ignominious fashion, caught by a cross-arm breaker and submitted in 26 seconds by the popular Kendo Kashin.

Teaming with his former RINGS colleague, Mitsuya Nagai, Naruse experienced moderate tag-team success, winning the All Asia Tag-Team Titles in 2004 but, despite a strong showing in the 2004 Best of the Super Juniors, further individual success eluded him and Naruse left pro-wrestling in 2006.

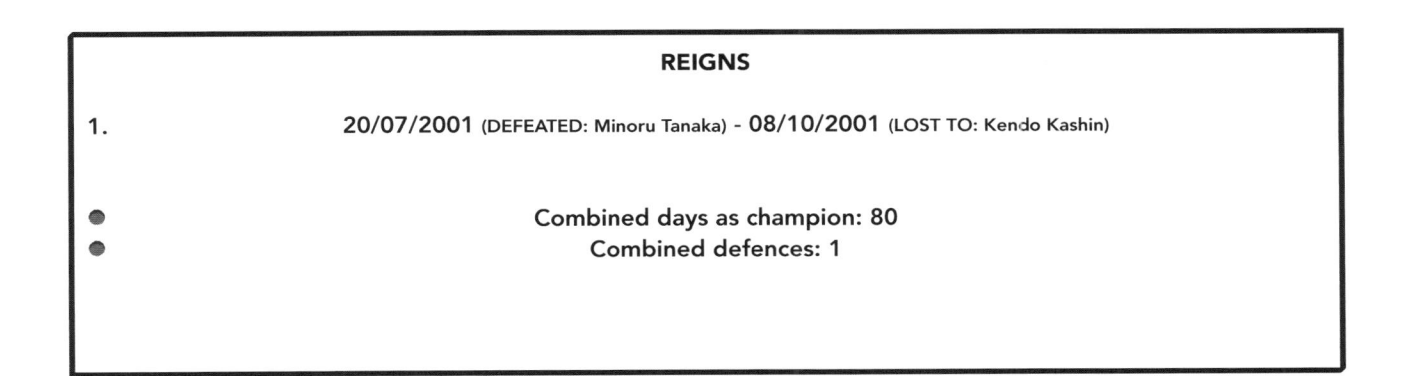

REIGNS
1.   20/07/2001 (DEFEATED: Minoru Tanaka) - 08/10/2001 (LOST TO: Kendo Kashin)
• Combined days as champion: 80
• Combined defences: 1

22. Tiger Mask IV

Yoshihiro Yamazaki was primarily trained for pro-wrestling by The Great Sasuke and the original Tiger Mask, Satoru Sayama, and he debuted under the Tiger Mask gimmick with Sayama's blessing for Sasuke's Michinoku Pro-Wrestling in 1995.

Lightning fast, utilising strikes, suplexes and submissions, this incarnation of Tiger Mask was a perfect fit for the wrestling landscape in Japan of the late nineties, as a Michinoku Pro wrestler he would appear for Battlarts, UFO, AAA, AJPW, Toryumon and the WWF before landing in New Japan in 2002.

Instantly positioned as a threat to the IWGP Jr. Heavyweight Championship, Tiger Mask unsuccessfully challenged Kanemoto in September 2002, but won the next time the two met in April of the following year to win the championship for the first time. Seemingly unbeatable in his five months as champion, Tiger Mask was stripped of his title to set up a Junior Heavyweight showcase Battle Royale at the Tokyo Dome in October 2003.

Winning the Best of the Super Juniors 2004 in emphatic fashion he went on to challenge Minoru "Heat" Tanaka in July; initially unsuccessful, it would be the rematch in the Tokyo Dome that would bring Tiger Mask victory and, once more, the IWGP Jr. Heavyweight Championship and the start of his longest reign. Feuding with Black Tiger as portrayed by Rocky Romero occupied 2005 and 2006 while a new generation of juniors entered New Japan, both from the dojo and from abroad as NJPW began to open itself to the world in order to grow. As the standard bearer for his generation and division, Tiger Mask would battle Devitt, Low-Ki and Místico, losing his final Junior Heavyweight Championship to the NOAH invader Naomichi Marufuji at the turn of the decade.

In the following years Tiger Mask held his head high, as the man who had spent the longest time under the moniker, gate keeper for the division and a noble contributor to the legacy of Tiger Mask which transcends companies and generations.

REIGNS

1. 23/04/2003 (DEFEATED: Koji Kanemoto) - 23/09/2003 (LOST TO: Vacated to be defended in Battle Royale)
2. 04/01/2005 (DEFEATED: Heat) - 08/10/2005 (LOST TO: Black Tiger)
3. 19/02/2006 (DEFEATED: Black Tiger) - 03/05/2006 (LOST TO: Koji Kanemoto)
4. 08/07/2008 (DEFEATED: Prince Devitt) - 21/09/2008 (LOST TO: Low Ki)
5. 04/01/2009 (DEFEATED: Low Ki) - 15/08/2009 (LOST TO: Místico)
6. 08/11/2009 (DEFEATED: Místico) - 04/01/2010 (LOST TO: Naomichi Marufuji)

- Combined days as champion: 858
- Combined defences: 12

23. Jado

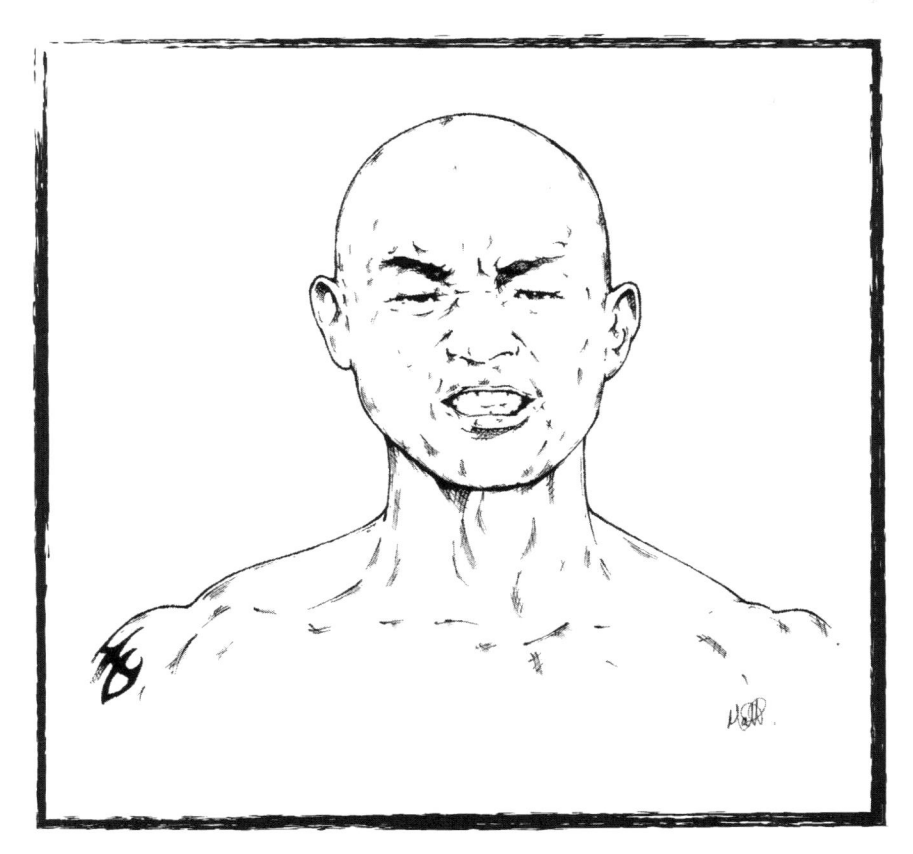

Debuting in 1989 for FMW, Shoji Akiyoshi soon moved to the UWF and became an integral part of the thrilling, heavily lucha libre inspired junior heavyweight scene of the time. Under the name Coolie SZ he began teaming with Bulldog KT and the two became inseparable, battling the best in the company and famous touring luchadores. Wrestling under his real name before becoming Punish (alongside Crush) the pair toured Mexico together extensively between 1991 and 1993, winning UWA Tag Gold as Jado and Gedo. The two were independent sensations, finding success with WING, WAR, FMW, BJW, AJPW among other companies before finally arriving in NJPW together as part of the NWO offshoot, Team 2000 in, fashionably late, June 2001.

Instantly credible the pair captured the Junior Tag Titles in July of the same year and held them until May 2002. Although Jado would enter Best of the Super Juniors as a singles competitor, he almost exclusively worked in the tag division and it was only via the Battle Royale held at the Tokyo Dome in October 2003 that Jado came into the IWGP Jr. Heavyweight Title picture. The numbers game worked for Jado as his allies Gedo and Dick Togo, alongside relentless acts of villainy, weakened Koji Kanemoto enough for him to tap out to Jado's Cross-face, making Jado the new champion. And he would be a double champion a month later as he and Gedo once more reclaimed the Junior Tag-Team Titles.

The glory days were short lived because as a singles competitor Jado was vastly over matched when he met Minoru "Heat" Tanaka in December, losing his singles gold in under ten minutes. Great wrestling minds, Jado and Gedo worked best together and many more years of joint success would follow.

REIGNS
1.   13/10/2003 (DEFEATED: Battle Royale winner) - 14/12/2003 (LOST TO: Minoru "Heat" Tanaka)
•   Combined days as champion: 62
•   Combined defences: 1

24. Black Tiger IV

Establishing a name for himself on the Californian independent wrestling scene in the late 90s, Rocky Romero was a veteran of five years when New Japan opened the Inoki Dojo in Santa Monica as a permanent base to scout foreign talent. Alongside such luminaries as Brian Danielson, Samoa Joe and Romero's long term tag partner Ricky Reyes, Rocky enrolled with the dojo which acted as both a finishing school and a springboard for his career.

In 2002 Rocky made his first tour with NJPW alongside Ricky Reyes as one half of the Havana Pitbulls and for the next few years continued to build his reputation as a hugely capable technician and a brilliant wrestling mind, working extensively in Mexico and the USA alongside frequent appearances for NJPW.

In 2005, Romero was chosen to be the forth incarnation of Black Tiger, which placed him in the orbit of the reinvigorated Tiger Mask of the day. In short order, Black Tiger re-established himself as the nemesis of Tiger Mask by aligning himself with Liger's CTU faction and in only the second one-on-one meeting between the two, in October 2005, defeated him to become IWGP Jr. Heavyweight Champion. The reign lasted four months before Tiger Mask regained the championship, but, the feud between the two being eternal, things did not end there.

For the next three years Romero travelled the world, notably working for NOAH, ROH and CMLL before returning to New Japan to once more challenge Tiger Mask for the Junior Heavyweight Title, this time putting his mask on the line. On suffering defeat, Black Tiger IV passed into the history books on the 5th of April 2009, but Rocky Romero lived on and would certainly be back to cause chaos in the future.

REIGNS
1.   08/10/2005 (DEFEATED: Tiger Mask IV) - 19/02/2006 (LOST TO: Tiger Mask IV)
Combined days as champion: 134
Combined defences: 1

25. Ryusuke Taguchi

A product of the NJPW dojo, Taguchi made his debt for New Japan at the end of 2002. An accomplished amateur wrestler, clad in standard issue black shorts with short hair, he formed a successful tag-team with fellow Young Lion, Hirooki Goto. He participated in two Best of the Super Juniors tournaments and won the 2004 Young Lion´s Cup before spending most of 2005 in Mexico with CMLL.

On his return, he won his first gold, teaming with El Samurai he became one half of the Junior Heavyweight Tag Champions battling the villainous CTU Unit. With gold around his waist, mid-length hair a fashionable beard and greater swagger, Taguchi really began to stand out. In his first match of his 2007 Best of the Super Juniors campaign he defeated the then IWGP Jr. Heavyweight Champion Minoru, earning the future right to challenge for the title. The match came to pass on the 6th of July 2007 with Taguchi winning and going on to have a strong five month reign.

A huge crowd favourite, his signature hip-attack a call back to the earliest days of the title's lineage, Taguchi was a wildly popular young man. Converting the previously evil Prince Devitt to the side of good, the two enjoyed great success as the tag-team Apollo 55, buoyed by which, Taguchi won the Best of the Super Juniors in 2012 though he was unsuccessful when challenging Low Ki for the IWGP Junior Championship. It would take the dissolution of his relationship with Devitt and the lengthy feud that resulted of it, to bring a harder, winning edge out of Taguchi, pushing him once more to the forefront of the division. Defeating Kushida to become champion in September 2014, Taguchi continued to be a force for good, battling the wrong doers in NJPW; successfully against Suzuki-Gun but falling to the newest Bullet Club recruit, Kenny Omega.

Over time, Taguchi figured less in contention for individual honours, focusing more on a role as a tag-team specialist, coach and enduring positive role model.

REIGNS

1. 06/07/2007 (DEFEATED: Minoru) - 08/12/2007 (LOST TO: Wataru Inoue)
2. 21/09/2014 (DEFEATED: Kushida) - 04/01/2015 (LOST TO: Kenny Omega)

- Combined days as champion: 260
- Combined defences: 6

26. Wataru Inoue

Inoue graduated from the New Japan dojo in late 1999, debuting for the company on the same Battle Royale as his contemporary and early rival Katsuyori Shibata. The two peerless technicians showed promise from day one and would soon start teaming together, even challenging Jado and Gedo for Junior Tag gold in 2001 and again in 2002.

With Shibata's departure in 2004, Inoue began teaming with legends El Samurai and Koji Kanemoto on a semi regular basis, winning his first championship, the IWGP Jr. Heavyweight Tag Team Titles, alongside the latter in early 2005.

Steadily rising in stature with the passing of the years, Inoue made it to the finals of the 2007 Best of the Super Juniors only to lose to Milano Collection A.T. His following bout, a tag title match alongside Kanemoto, also ended in defeat and Inoue took time away to assess his situation and develop further.

Returning from Mexico four months later, a sharper, refined and physically bigger Inoue set his sights on then junior champion Taguchi, defeating him on the 8th of December 2007 to claim the championship. Newly dominant, Inoue achieved the remarkable feat of entering and winning the 2008 Best of the Super Juniors tournament whilst the division's champion and, on the night after the finals, he vacated the Junior Heavyweight Championship, in search of further challenges in the heavyweight division.

REIGNS
1. 08/12/2007 (DEFEATED: Ryusuke Taguchi) - 16/06/2008 (LOST TO: Vacated to move to heavyweight division)
• Combined days as champion: 191
• Combined defences: 3

27. Low ki

Emerging from New Jersey in the late nineties, Low Ki quickly gained renown for his vicious kicks and thrilling move set, becoming a name on the US independent scene with an aura of legitimate toughness. A leading light in the explosion in the popularity of independent wrestling, Low Ki was the first ever ROH champion and the second ever X-Division champion in NWA/TNA when he made his first appearance in Japan, for ZERO-1 in 2002. Defeating Brian Kendrick on said tour, Low Ki became the second ever ZERO-1 International Junior Heavyweight Champion and the world seemed to be his for the taking.

Low Ki spent much of the following five years in Japan, finally debuting for NJPW in late 2007 as a member of RISE, but would not return until September 2008 when it was seen that he had defected to the villainous GBH stable. This put him on the opposite side of the IWGP Jr. Heavyweight Champion Tiger Mask, each match of the tour saw Low Ki assault Tiger Mask mercilessly, culminating in Low Ki defeating him on the penultimate day of the tour to become the new champion; the reign lasted until the Tokyo Dome in January where Tiger Mask regained his title, after which Low Ki went to WWE.

2012 was the year that saw Low Ki spend his longest time in New Japan. Following his stint with WWE, he was unquestionably a bigger international star and was placed in instant Junior Championship contention, both for individual honours and alongside his long time, fellow Jersey associate, Homicide, to challenge for tag titles. In both instances he would clash with Prince Devitt, defeating him in May for his second Junior Heavyweight Championship which he would hold until July. He and Ibushi would then trade the title back and forth until Prince Devitt finally defeated Low Ki to reclaim the championship, going on to retain it in the latter´s final NJPW match to date at the Tokyo Dome, January 2013.

REIGNS

1. 21/09/2008 (DEFEATED: Tiger Mask IV) - 04/01/2009 (LOST TO: Tiger Mask IV)
2. 03/05/2012 (DEFEATED: Prince Devitt) - 29/07/2012 (LOST TO: Kota Ibushi)
3. 08/10/2012 (DEFEATED: Kota Ibushi) - 11/11/2012 (LOST TO: Prince Devitt)

- Combined days as champion: 226
- Combined defences: 2

28. Místico

Following the family tradition, Luis Ignacio Urive Alvirde began wrestling at the age of 15 in Mexico City, making his debut for CMLL three years later in the summer of 2000. 2004 saw CMLL give him the character of Místico, an orphan taught to wrestle by the famed wrestling priest Fray Tormenta; teaming with the established técnicos the young Místico was given a chance to taste victory and demonstrate spectacular high flying skills against the top rudos.

By 2009, Místico was the biggest draw in all Mexico and had been for several years and it was in this capacity that he appeared as a special attraction guest at NJPW´s 3rd Wrestle Kingdom show at the Tokyo Dome. Fans were utterly in awe of Místico´s spectacular aura and he was invited back in February to defend his own CMLL Welterweight Championship, then again in August to challenge Tiger Mask for the IWGP Jr. Heavyweight Championship. A challenge which Místico more than rose to, winning the belt and taking it back to Mexico, where his two successful defences took place.

On his return to Japan in November, Místico dropped the championship back to Tiger Mask, but, despite this defeat, he would remain revered in the coming years, being one of the central figures in the creation of the annual CMLL/ NJPW Fantasticamania shows which remain a highlight of the NJPW calendar to this day.

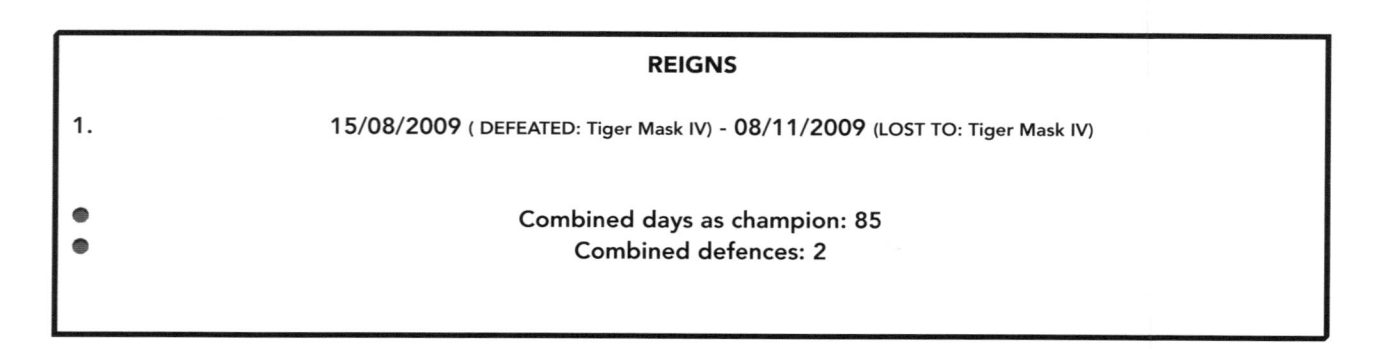

REIGNS
1. 15/08/2009 (DEFEATED: Tiger Mask IV) - 08/11/2009 (LOST TO: Tiger Mask IV)
Combined days as champion: 85 Combined defences: 2

29. Naomichi Marufuji

By mid-2009, Naomichi Marufuji had already won every accolade available to him in NOAH, including that of GHC Heavyweight Champion. Additionally, he had also won the All Japan World Jr. Heavyweight Championship and had recently acquired the position of vice president of Pro-Wrestling NOAH following the tragic death of Misawa. Marufuji was already a legend and a top contender wherever he appeared and in 2009 he re-appeared in New Japan having had only three previous matches for the company across 2003/4.

Defeating Liger, Taguchi and Tiger Mask to reach the finals of the 2009 Super J-Cup, Marufuji finished the job by toppling Prince Devitt on the 23rd December 2009 to book a spot against the IWGP Junior Heavyweight Champion at the Tokyo Dome in January. The NOAH icon promptly defeated Tiger Mask IV and took the championship back with him, appearing in New Japan on a monthly basis solely to defend his title until his packed schedule finally became too much for him, Marufuji eventually lost the championship to a fresh and focused Prince Devitt in June 2010.

With his championship reign, Marufuji became the first man to have won the IWGP, GHC and AJPW World Jr. Heavyweight Championships, earning the right to be forever considered the Universal Junior Ace.

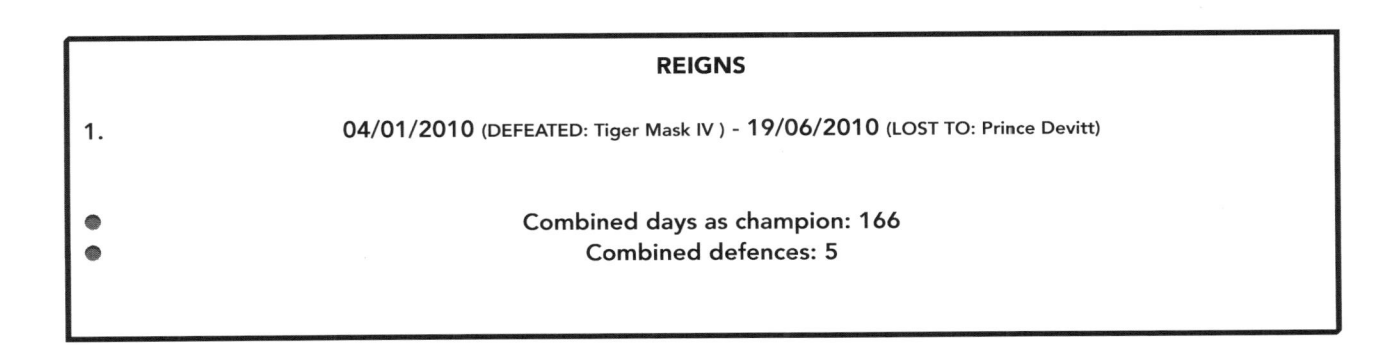

REIGNS
1.   04/01/2010 (DEFEATED: Tiger Mask IV) - 19/06/2010 (LOST TO: Prince Devitt)
Combined days as champion: 166 Combined defences: 5

30. Prince Devitt

Starting his wrestling career in England, coming through the NWA UK Hammerlock training system, the then Fergal Devitt carried himself with an air of professionalism to accompany his pure wrestling acumen to suggest that he would always make it big. Debuting in 2000, he acquired titles quickly and displayed great entrepreneurship by opening an NWA affiliated wrestling company in his home town of Bray, Ireland.

As NWA British Commonwealth Champion, Devitt was invited to compete in the U.S for the NWA on a number of occasions; following one such instance in 2005 he was invited to attend the Inoki Dojo in California, bringing him into contact with New Japan for the first time. Making a dazzling impression on his trainers, he was invited to continue his training in Tokyo, debuting for the company under the new name of Prince Devitt in March 2006.

It would be as a team player that Devitt established himself as a contender within the junior ranks, first as a member of Liger´s CTU, then teaming with Minoru in RISE before forming Apollo 55 with Taguchi and by mid-2010 he was a three time Jr. Tag-Team Champion. 2010 was very much Devitt´s year, he won the Best of the Super Juniors tournament, leading to him challenging and beating Marufuji for his first reign as IWGP Jr. Heavyweight Champion, then he participated in the G1, scoring a huge win over Tanahashi and was constantly at the forefront of the best of what the company was offering. This first reign lasted one day short of a year, his second lasted 8 months, his third a staggering 14 months.

It was during this final reign that Devitt founded The Bullet Club and showed himself to be a wrestler that transcended weight classes, stating repeatedly that he wished to be the first wrestler to hold the IWGP Junior and Heavyweight Titles at the same time. In thrilling matches with Okada and Tanahashi he more than showed himself capable of doing just that, yet fell short in his heavyweight ambitions. In the end, Devitt was destroyed by his own creation, The Bullet Club turning on him and pushing him out of the company in April as he battled Taguchi one last time, having already lost the Junior Heavyweight Championship to Ibushi at the Tokyo Dome 2014.

REIGNS

1. 19/06/2010 (DEFEATED: Naomichi Marufuji) - 18/06/2011 (LOST TO: Kota Ibushi)
2. 19/09/2011 (DEFEATED: Kushida) - 03/05/2012 (LOST TO: Low Ki)
3. 11/11/2012 (DEFEATED: Low Ki) - 04/01/2014 (LOST TO: Kota Ibushi)

- Combined days as champion: 1,010
- Combined defences: 15

31. Kota Ibushi

Moving from karate to pro-wrestling, Ibushi debuted for DDT Pro-Wrestling in July 2004 at the age of 22. Incredibly photogenic, jaw droppingly athletic and a legitimate tough guy, Ibushi appeared on the NJPW radar very quickly and had several tag-matches on New Japan developmental shows in late 2004/early 2005. However, the next few years saw him steal shows across the Japanese independent spectrum from DDT to Battlarts, Michinoku Pro to NOAH and everywhere in between.

August 2008 saw the first arrival in Japan of Kenny Omega; though initially foes, Kenny and Kota quickly formed a tag-team, the sensational Golden Lovers and their success proved a catalyst for Ibushi's singles career. In March 2009 Ibushi won the Rey de Voladores tournament run by the U.S independent promotion Chikara and in May of the same year returned to New Japan, reaching the semi final of the Best of the Super Juniors, losing an intense war with Prince Devitt. The following year saw him go one further, reaching the final before once more falling to Devitt, but in October Ibushi gained a measure of revenge as he and Omega bested Devitt and Taguchi for the Junior Tag-Team titles. The feud between Devitt and Ibushi was escalated to the Tokyo Dome and the two greeted 2011 with a classic match that once more saw Ibushi defeated, this time in a match for a Junior Heavyweight Championship. Not to be denied Ibushi once more went on to go one step further in 2011, winning Best of the Super Juniors and finally defeating Devitt to become IWGP Junior Heavyweight Champion.

Sadly his first reign would be cut short after a dislocated shoulder in September necessitated vacating the title, keeping Ibushi away from NJPW until June 2012 when he promptly challenged and soon after defeated Low Ki to start his second reign. Dividing his time between New Japan and DDT, Ibushi wrestled on the grandest of stages for NJPW, taking breathtaking risk for the ultimate rewards. His final IWGP Junior title reign starting as he vanquished Devitt at the Tokyo Dome once more, yet ended in July 2014 with a concussion following a loss to Kushida. The Golden Star continued to ascend and burn bright in the heavyweight division, utterly unique and truly irreplaceable.

REIGNS

1. 18/06/2011 (DEFEATED: Prince Devitt) - 12/09/2011 (LOST TO: Vacated due to injury)
2. 29/07/2012 (DEFEATED: Low Ki) - 08/10/2012 (LOST TO: Low Ki)
3. 04/01/2014 (DEFEATED: Prince Devitt) - 04/07/2014 (LOST TO: Kushida)

- Combined days as champion: 337
- Combined defences: 8

32. Kushida

During Junior High school, Yujiro Kushida attended Takada Dojo and was simultaneously trained in both MMA and Pro-Wrestling. Despite early promise in MMA, Kushida opted for a pro-wrestling career and made his Japanese pro-wrestling debut for Takada´s HUSTLE promotion.

Working extensively for a wide range of promotions, national and international ranging from All Japan to Osaka Pro and a host of Canadian companies, Kushida represented HUSTLE´s spiritual successor SMASH in the 2010 installment of the Best of the Super Juniors in New Japan. A spirited performance prefaced Kushida´s joining NJPW full time in 2011, challenging, albeit unsuccessfully, for the IWJP Jr. Heavyweight Championship in March of that year during the 39th Anniversary Tour.

Toiling in multi-man matches outside of performances in Best of the Super Juniors, Kushida was truly catalysed by a brief return to the States in August 2012 where he formed a bond with Alex Shelley. The two clicked instantly as tag-partners and with the name Time Splitters won the first of their two Junior Tag Championships in November 2012. Dominating the junior tag ranks, Kushida still participated in Best of the Super Juniors, reaching the finals in 2014 which signified his arrival as a true singles star. Two weeks after losing the final to Ricochet, Kushida defeated Ibushi to win the Junior Heavyweight Championship for the first time, making him a double champ as the Time Splitters were already Junior tag team champions. Though he lost to Taguchi on his first defence Kushida had arrived at the forefront of the division and almost exactly the same pattern was replicated the following year but with the added distinction of winning Best of the Super Juniors, again there was victory in July and defeat in September.

2016 was Kushida´s full year on top, fully recognised as the Ace of the division a beloved star who had achieved everything possible in New Japan, he began to take greater pleasure in working a range of International dates throughout 2017/18 with NJPW´s partners ROH and RPW before announcing his departure for WWE in 2019.

REIGNS

1. 04/07/2014 (DEFEATED: Kota Ibushi) - 21/09/2014 (LOST TO: Ryusuke Taguchi)
2. 05/07/2015 (DEFEATED: Kenny Omega) - 23/09/2015 (LOST TO: Kenny Omega)
3. 04/01/2016 (DEFEATED: Kenny Omega) - 17/09/2016 (LOST TO: Bushi)
4. 05/11/2016 (DEFEATED: Bushi) - 04/01/2017 (LOST TO: Hiromu Takahashi)
5. 11/06/2017 (DEFEATED: Hiromu Takahashi) - 09/10/2017 (LOST TO: Will Ospreay)
6. 08/10/2018 (DEFEATED: Marty Scurll) - 04/01/2019 (LOST TO: Taiji Ishimori)

- Combined days as champion: 684
- Combined defences: 8

33. Kenny Omega

Debuting at the age of 17 in his native Winnipeg, Canada in 2000, Omega won his first junior championship, the Canadian Unified Junior Title, just over six months after his first match, an auspicious start to an incredible career.

Subsequent years saw him mix with the best independent talent in Canada and spend a number of months with the WWE developmental promotion Deep South Wrestling, which opened more doors to the broader North American independent scene and led Omega to evaluate how best to progress within the world of wrestling.

2008 saw Omega debut for the Japanese promotion DDT Pro-Wrestling, where he was able to fulfil a personal ambition to fight against and then alongside maverick genius Kota Ibushi. As a tag-team, the Golden Lovers attracted a lot of attention with their high flying innovation and it was not long before New Japan showed interest in the tandem. In 2010 Omega appeared in New Japan's Best of the Super Juniors, dividing his time between Canadian and other North American independents with NJPW and DDT Pro. In September, Omega unsuccessfully challenged for the IWGP Jr. Heavyweight Championship for the first time, before defeating Apollo 55 alongside Ibushi to become IWGP Jr. Tag Team Champions.

2011 to 2014 saw Omega spend more and more time in Japan, winning gold with DDT and AJPW while annually participating in the Best of the Super Juniors Tournament. It was announced at the end of 2014 that Kenny had signed full time with New Japan and was named as Taguchi's challenger for the IWGP Jr. Heavyweight Championship at the January Tokyo Dome show. Affiliated with the Bullet Club, Omega debuted "The Cleaner" persona, an austere, yet comedic villain that saw Omega struggle to define himself in his new promotion. He defeated Taguchi for his first of two Junior Heavyweight reigns, but would truly unlock his full potential by assuming leadership of the Bullet Club and moving up to heavyweight the following year.

REIGNS
1. 04/01/2015 (DEFEATED: Ryusuke Taguchi) - 05/07/2015 (LOST TO: Kushida)
2. 23/09/2015 (DEFEATED: Kushida) - 04/01/2016 (LOST TO: Kushida)
Combined days as champion: 285
Combined defences: 4

34. Bushi

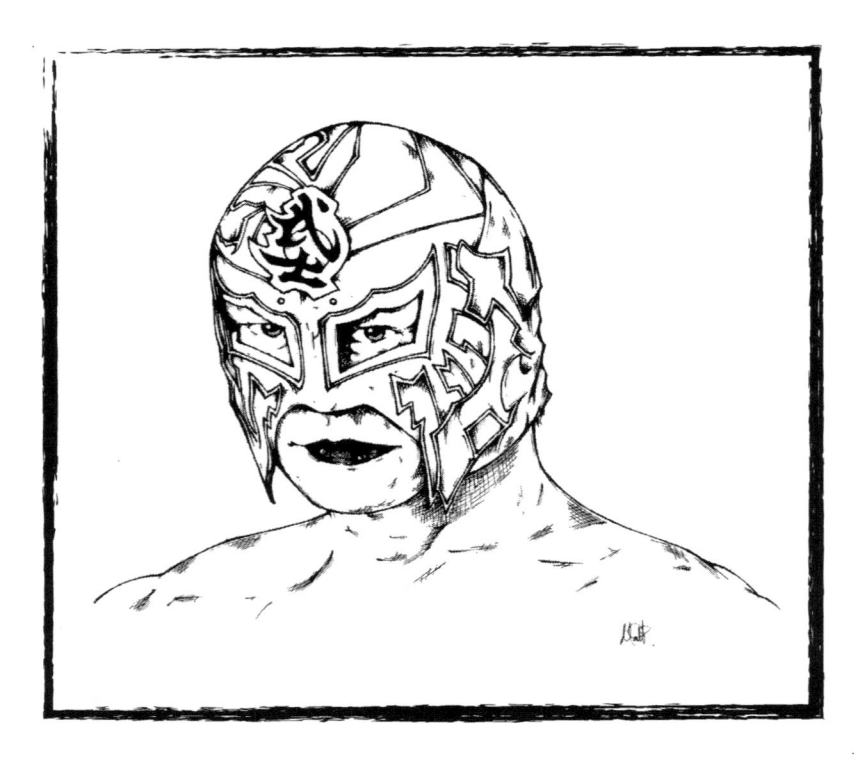

Trained by Animal Hamaguchi, Tetsuya Shimizu debuted under the name T28 for All Japan in spring 2007 and experienced a relatively rapid ascent. Within a few months this young junior was sharing the ring with the likes of Kensuke Sasaki and Keiji Muto and within the year had won the AJPW under 30 tag team tournament alongside his partner Kushida. Yet it was here that T28´s momentum stalled and much of the remainder of 2008 was spent on the losing end of his matches, things changing as he embarked on his learning excursion to Mexico, adopting the ring name Bushi and wrestling for the IWRG promotion.

Bushi retuned to AJPW rejuvenated and, alongside Super Crazy, won the 2010 Junior Tag League, but never received a true chance to shine as a solo performer. In May 2012 Bushi debuted for New Japan as part of the Best of the Super Juniors, somewhat continuing the role of a utility player in the junior division, there was no immediate top tier push for the masked grappler. 2012 saw him tag with Kushida, until the success of the Time Splitters left Bushi to drift alone; teaming sporadically with veterans and debuting young lions, Bushi was struggling once more to make inroads as a singles star.

Ironically, it would be misfortune that would lead to his greater success. Suffering severe injuries, including an epidural hematoma and extensive nerve damage in a match at the Korakuen Hall on 19th of December 2014 and then breaking his orbital bone during rehabilitation, Bushi was away from the ring for almost a year. When he returned, it was as the third member of the white-hot, cool heel faction, Los Ingobernables de Japon and as the group´s only junior heavyweight he set about building a feud with the then champion, Kushida. The two men, whose careers had intertwined for much of the previous decade, met on September the 17th in Tokyo with Bushi claiming victory and his one IWGP Junior Heavyweight Championship. With or without the championship, as part of Los Ingobernables, the wandering warrior Bushi had finally found where he belonged.

REIGNS
1.   17/09/2016 (DEFEATED: Kushida) - 05/11/2016 (LOST TO: Kushida)
Combined days as champion: 49
Combined defences: 0

35. Hiromu Takahashi

Graduating from the NJPW dojo at the age of 20, Takahashi debuted in the typical fashion of young lions, with shorn hair, black trunks and a defeat. It would take 6 months for Takahashi to earn a singles victory, notably in an entertaining feud with a dynamic young man from another promotion, Kazuki Hirata of DDT Pro.

A top prospect with an innate connection with the audience, Takahashi continued to gain experience on the undercard and via tournament appearances before departing first to England and then Mexico on his learning excursion in June 2013. Although, in this case, excursion is not quite the right word, because Takahashi spent nearly three years with CMLL, experiencing great success and engaging in a legendary feud with Dragon Lee over the CMLL World Lightweight Title. It was this feud that forged a dynamic risk taker out of the promising young lion, wrestling under the masked persona Kamaitachi he really came to embody the malevolent whirlwind spirit that lent him his name.

Hiromu Takahashi returned to New Japan on November the 5th 2016, walking out to challenge Kushida for his IWGP Junior Heavyweight Championship in a match that would take place in the Tokyo Dome that coming January. Aligning himself with Los Ingobernables de Japon, when the match came, Hiromu Takahashi took risks beyond the metal of the technician Kushida and won the match to become champion for the first time. An extravagant reign followed, Takahashi´s glowing character almost as much of a focus as his in-ring work, ending as Kushida reclaimed the title for himself in June.

2018 saw Takahashi truly emerge as one of the most popular men in the company. Spectacular victory in Best of the Super Juniors was swiftly followed by his becoming champion once more, though this reign was cut short in tragic circumstances. Battling his old rival Dragon Lee, Takahashi landed sickeningly on the top of his head, causing severe neck injuries and necessitating the title to be vacated, throwing his long term future within the sport into severe doubt. All of which making his effervescent return and his third reign as champion in 2020 an even more remarkable achievement.

REIGNS

1. 04/01/2017 (DEFEATED: Kushida) - 11/06/2017 (LOST TO: Kushida)
2. 09/06/2018 (DEFEATED: Will Ospreay) - 20/08/2018 (LOST TO: Vacated due to injury)
3. 04/01/2020 (DEFEATED: Will Ospreay) - 29/08/2020 (LOST TO : Taiji Ishimori)

- Combined days as champion: 468
- Combined defences: 7

36. Will Ospreay

Londoner Ospreay was first trained by the London School of Lucha Libre and blossomed in the burlesque tinted promotion where breathtaking athleticism was combined with a macabre fantasy aesthetic. Rapidly gaining attention on the U.K. scene, Ospreay became a spectacular fixture for Progress, Rev Pro and IPW U.K. earning him the opportunity to battle the top names on the national level and the biggest international stars passing through. 2015 saw Ospreay invited to California to appear for PWG in their annual Battle of Los Angeles tournament, making it to the semifinal, the tournament marked Ospreay´s grand coming out on the international stage.

In 2016 Will Ospreay made his first appearance for New Japan. Representing CHAOS, following a challenge made via video, Ospreay unsuccessfully challenged IWGP Jr. Heavyweight Champion Kushida. Despite the loss, Ospreay was established as a phenomenal athlete and a force to be reckoned with, so his entry in the 2016 Best of the Super Juniors tournament was greeted with enthusiasm. Not only did he win the tournament, but his spectacular style ignited debate across the industry regarding the very evolution of wrestling. In his subsequent championship challenge the iconoclast was defeated once more by Kushida, as he was when the two met again in the final of the 2017 Best of the Super Junior Tournament. On 9th October 2017, Kushida and Ospreay met once more, but this time Ospreay emerged triumphant to become the Junior Heavyweight Champion.

Losing the belt almost immediately to Marty Scurll, only offered the chance for Ospreay´s second reign to begin on the greatest stage, as he was victorious at the Tokyo Dome to regain the title. During this second reign, Ospreay expanded his repertoire, becoming more physical while maintaining his aerial abilities, he began to battle heavyweights on a more regular basis and pushed the reigning heavyweight champion, Okada, to his limit at the 2018 anniversary show. This theme continued in 2019, widely acknowledged as one of the greatest wrestlers of the modern era, having won his second Best of the Super Juniors and his third IWGP Jr. Heavyweight Championship, Ospreay was entered into the, G1 tournament to push the field to even greater heights and begin his transition away from the Junior division.

REIGNS

1. 09/10/2017 (DEFEATED: Kushida) - 05/11/2017 (LOST TO: Marty Scurll)
2. 04/01/2018 (DEFEATED: Kushida, Marty Scurll and Hiromu Takahashi) - 09/06/2018 (LOST TO: Hiromu Takahashi)
3. 09/06/2019 (DEFEATED: Dragon Lee)- 04/01/2020 (LOST TO: Hiromu Takahashi)

- Combined days as champion: 392
- Combined defences: 6

37. Marty Scurll

Initially trained by Dropkixx Pro-Wrestling in the south of England, Marty Scurll debuted for the promotion in 2005 and quickly established himself as a proficient technician; branching out in the first few years of his career to work for a wide range of UK independent promotions such as IPW UK and All Star promotions he was trusted at a very early stage to rub shoulders with touring stars passing thorough. A key figure in a resurgent, burgeoning UK independent scene as one half of the Leaders of the New School tag team with Zack Sabre Jr. and as a singles star as Party Marty. A huge evolutionary step took place in July 2014 as Marty grew out a devilish beard , started sporting an umbrella and began to be known as the villain.

Replete with his distinctive new look, Marty made his USA debut at the influential Battle of Los Angeles in 2015, making the semifinal in his first appearance and going on to win the tournament the following year. Appearances with New Japan affiliated companies RPW and ROH opened the path to Japan for Marty and he debuted in the Korakuen with a victory over Will Ospreay as part of the Best of the Super Juniors 2017. Though he failed to win the tournament, the idea that Scurll had a hex over Ospreay persisted and was the foundation behind the Scurll´s November 2017 challenge for Ospreay´s Jr. Heavyweight Championship, which he won by grounding the aerialist in admirable fashion, becoming champion in the process.

This singular reign was short lived, defeat at the Tokyo Dome soon followed, but the inexorable march of progress continued for Scurll as his popularity steadily grew, leading him to become a true international star, breaking away from the Bullet Club to establish Villain Enterprises in late 2018.

REIGNS
1.   05/11/2017 (DEFEATED: Will Ospreay) - 04/01/2018 (LOST TO: Will Ospreay)
Combined days as champion: 60
Combined defences: 0

38. Taiji Ishimori

Receiving his initial training from Último Dragón as part of Toryumon Mexico, Ishimori started his career at a sprint. Within a year of his May 2002 debut, he had won the Young Dragon´s Cup, the Yamaha Cup and the UWA World Welterweight Title.

Moving through the Inoki dojo, Ishimori first appeared for NJPW in the Autumn of 2004, teaming with his trainer Último Dragón to challenge Jado and Gedo for the IWGP Jr. Heavyweight Tag titles. A six month run with the company followed, during which time he would team with fellow youngster Hiroshi Tanahashi to win a one night under-30 tag-tournament raising his stock with every match.

Late 2005 saw Ishimori move to AJPW and then land in NOAH in 2006 which is where he truly made his name, becoming the jewel in the crown of their Junior Heavyweight division, he spent twelve years wrestling on the emerald green mat, achieving every goal he set himself.

On May 4th 2018, Ishimori shocked the world by aligning himself with the Bullet Club under the guise of Bone Soldier and returning full time to New Japan. He blazed a trail immediately on his return, making his way to the final of the 2018 Best of the Super Juniors, remaining a hugely impressive figure even in defeat. Toward the end of the year he began to target the legendary Kushida, goading him into a match at the Tokyo Dome for the IWGP Jr. Heavyweight Championship; Ishimori won a classic, only to lose the title as New Japan spread its wings to the United States, with Ishimori´s first reign ending as he stared up at the lights in Madison Square Garden. In the summer of 2020, Ishimori went to war with Hiromu Takahashi, capturing the Junior Heavyweight Championship for a second time in the memorable open-air event held in the Meiji Jingu Stadium.

REIGNS

1. 04/01/2019 (DEFEATED: Kushida) - 06/04/2019 (LOST TO: Dragon Lee)
2. 29/08/2020 (DEFEATED: Hiromu Takahashi) - (CURRENT)

- Combined days as champion: 174+
- Combined defences: 2+

39. Dragon Lee

From a wrestling family, Dragon Lee inherited his ring name from his brother, who had moved on to adopt the Místico name, and made his in ring debut for CMLL on New Year's day 2014. By the end of his first hugely successful year, two greatly significant things had occurred to shape his career going forward. The first being that he had established himself as a contender for the CMLL World Lightweight Title and the second being that he had had his first matches with Hiromu Takahashi, working under the name Kamaitachi while he was on loan from NJPW. Dragon Lee became Lightweight Champion in April 2015 and spent the following year engaged in an exhilarating, daredevil feud, trading the title back and forth with Takahashi.

The feud forged both men and would come to define them; when Takahashi returned to Japan and claimed the IWGP Jr. Heavyweight Championship, Dragon Lee followed him and became his first challenger, both men shocking the Osaka crowd with the lengths to which they pushed themselves in pursuit of victory. Similarly breathtaking matches took place during the 2017 and 2018 Best of the Super Juniors tournaments, both times Dragon Lee emerging victorious.

Dragon Lee´s time would finally come on the ground breaking April 2019 show in Madison Square Garden, overcoming Bandido and the reigning champion Taiji Ishimori to become IWGP Jr. Heavyweight Champion. Despite losing the belt just two months later, Dragon Lee is a hugely popular international talent just entering his prime, who is destined to be around, scaling new heights, for many years to come.

REIGNS

1. 06/04/2019 (DEFEATED: Bandido and Taiji Ishimori) - 09/06/2019 (LOST TO: Will Ospreay)

Combined days as champion: 79
Combined defences: 1

CLASSIC MATCH N°2

Date: 17th February 2017
Location: EDION Arena, Osaka
Attendance: 5,466

DRAGON LEE vs HIROMU TAKAHASHI

Taking flight and pushing the limits of what the human body is capable of. Another pair of star crossed rivals, Takahashi and Lee setting new standards in defence and pursuit of the IWGP Junior Heavyweight Championship.

AJPW WORLD JR. HEAVYWEIGHT CHAMPIONSHIP

On December the 10th, 1979 in Los Angeles, California, a match was promoted between Chavo Guerrero, a well respected former NWA World Light Heavyweight Champion with experience of Japan with both, AJPW and NJPW and Steve Keirn, an NWA star in Florida who also had experience with All Japan. The match was to crown the inaugural NWA International Jr. Heavyweight Champion, Kiern won the battle and went on tour with New Japan, within two months losing the belt to then WWF Jr. Heavyweight Champion Tatsunami Fujinami in a match where both titles were on the line. Defended between NJPW and the United States over the following year, this ended with the reign of Les Thornton, who took the belt from New Japan to Florida, where it finally found its way into the hands of Chavo Guerrero.

Guerrero was persuaded by Giant Baba to switch his Japanese allegiances from New to All Japan in an attempt to capture the popularity of New Japan´s vibrant junior division being led by Fujinami, Tiger Mask and the Dynamite Kid. Making his return to the country in August 1981, Guerrero became the first man to defend the title in AJPW when he did so against Dos Caras the following month. When Atsushi Onita, the first graduate of the All Japan dojo and hand picked domestic junior ace defeated Guerrero in 1982 and defended the title against Halcón Ortiz in Mexico City, he returned with it to Japan and the practice of sharing its defence with other companies was ceased, All Japan becoming sole custodian of its lineage. The final NWA International Jr. Heavyweight Champion for 22 years would be Tiger Mask II (Mitsuharu Misawa) who won the title in August 1985 and whose reign lasted almost a year until he vacated it in order to move to the heavyweight division in June 1986, with the title being decommissioned.

Convergence is a phenomenon occurring in nature where unrelated species of plants or animals evolve similarly when placed in similar environmental conditions and so it was with All and New Japan´s junior divisions. Just five months after a tournament was held to crown the first IWGP Jr. Heavyweight Champion, a tournament was held in July 1986 to crown the first AJPW World Jr. Heavyweight Champion, with Hiro Saito claiming the honour. Though the World Jr. Heavyweight Championship has struggled for the spotlight over the years, it has been held by some of the most gifted wrestlers of all time who have produced battles over it worthy of being considered the best of any promotion and any weight class in any era and remains to this day a cherished championship of true worth.

1. Hiro Saito

Graduating from the NJPW dojo, Saito debuted at the age of 17 for New Japan in 1978, enduring years of singles defeats in learning his craft, his first victory came over Norio Honaga in April 1980. In 1982, Saito left on his learning excursion, first spending time with the UWA in Mexico and then a year in Calgary with Stampede Wrestling, where he adopted the Senton Splash, becoming the first Japanese wrestler to popularise its use when he returned in 1984.

In the 8 months that he spent with NJPW following his return, Saito captured the WWF Jr. Heavyweight Title from his Calgary tag team partner, The Cobra, losing it back to him on the 28th of July before returning to Stampede and ultimately jumping to AJPW. Grouped with wrestlers who also had experience with Stampede, Saito formed the Calgary Hurricanes.

Exactly one year into his time with AJPW, Saito fought the respected American technician Brad Armstrong for the newly activated AJPW World Jr. Heavyweight Championship, winning the match to be crowned the inaugural champion. Holding the title until November, Saito would have one unsuccessful attempt at winning the title back by challenging Masanobu Fuchi in March 1987, before returning to New Japan in May where he would remain for much of the rest of his career.

REIGNS
1.   31/07/1986 (DEFEATED: Brad Armstrong) - 23/11/1986 (LOST TO: Kuniaki Kobayashi)
• Combined days as champion: 115
• Combined defences: 3

2. Kuniaki Kobayashi

Returning to New Japan following a lengthy overseas excursion with UWA in Mexico and NWA territories in the USA, Kuniaki Kobayashi was treated as a top contender for the WWF Jr. Heavyweight Title. Engaging in a series of matches across 1982 and 1983 with both Tiger Mask (Sayama) and Dynamite Kid, Kobashi truly made his name as a handsome, athletic hot-head, keeping up with his iconic opponents physically but often losing via disqualification, unable to keep his animosity for them within the rules. Joining the villainous faction Ishin Gundan, Kobayashi continued to battle New Japan´s heroes until he and the rest of the faction followed Riki Choshu to form new promotion JPW in 1984, which in turn invaded AJPW in 1985.

In All Japan, Kobayashi´s great rivalries continued, battling both Dynamite Kid and Tiger Mask, though the latter now portrayed by Misawa, he would defeat Dynamite to win the NWA International Jr. Heavyweight title in June 1985, before losing it to the final champion, Tiger Mask, in August.

As the new year began, Kobayashi fought the legendary Mil Mascaras to a double count-out in pursuit of the IWA World Heavyweight Title and then in September 1986 was the second man to unsuccessfully challenge Hiro Saito for the newly minted AJPW World Jr. Heavyweight Championship. However, at his second attempt in November, Kobayashi eventually overcame Saito to claim the title for himself. His reign was relatively short, just over a month, and entirely centred around the elevation of home-grown junior heavyweight Masanobu Fuchi, who captured the belt from Kobayashi in January 1987. By summer, Ishin Gundan had returned to NJPW, where Kobayashi spent the rest of his career.

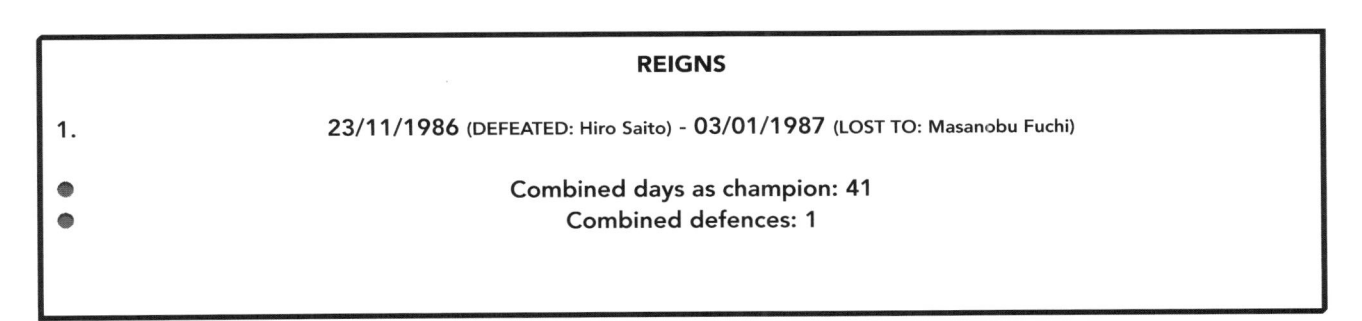

REIGNS
1.   23/11/1986 (DEFEATED: Hiro Saito) - 03/01/1987 (LOST TO: Masanobu Fuchi)
Combined days as champion: 41
Combined defences: 1

3. Masanobu Fuchi

Among the first trainees to graduate from the AJPW dojo, taught by the trinity of Baba, Gotch and Dick Beyer, Fuchi debuted in July 1974, spending much of his first year in battle with fellow graduate Atsushi Onita. Tough all-rounders, the two toiled for six years on the undercard for AJPW before being sent on excursion to the States where they worked as a tag team in the Memphis and Florida territories. In early 1982, Onita was recalled by AJPW to be the centrepiece of the New Jr. Heavyweight division, allowing Fuchi to travel through the Carolinas on his own, gaining invaluable experience against the likes of Dory Funk Jr., Ricky Steamboat and Ric Flair before himself being recalled in July 1983.

Fuchi´s first and only attempt at the NWA International Jr. heavyweight Title, was a losing effort against Chavo Guerrero a mere month following his return and he would have to wait three years, in which time Onita was forced to retire (for the first time) and Tiger Mask became a heavyweight, before getting a shot at the AJPW World Jr. Title. Despite defeating Saito via disqualification, the champion retained, similarly, in December, though not pinned or submitted the referee decreed Fuchi could not continue against the rule breaking Kuniyaki.

Fuchi was portrayed as a gutsy hero with the deck stacked against him and the crowd were overjoyed when he finally overcame those odds in the Korakuen Hall in January 1987 to win the title for the first time. This first reign lasted two years, until he was finally overcome by Joe Malenko; 1989 saw a spasm of short reigns by potential leaders of the division, five men with none holding the belt much more than a month and when the title finally found its way back to Fuchi he held it for the following four years. Masanobu Fuchi was a dependable standard bearer for the junior division, a master story teller, and staunchly loyal to All Japan. Following the exodus to NOAH, Fuchi was one of only two Japanese wrestlers to remain in the company, at that time taking on significant managerial role alongside his work as an active wrestler. To date, he last challenged for the AJPW World Jr. Heavyweight Championship in December 2014, over 40 years since his debut, an incredible man.

REIGNS

1. 03/01/1987 (DEFEATED: Kuniaki Kobayashi) - 20/01/1989 (LOST TO: Joe Malenko)
2. 08/03/1989 (DEFEATED: Mighty Inoue) - 26/04/1989 (LOST TO: Shinichi Nakano)
3. 20/10/1989 (DEFEATED: Joe Malenko) - 21/05/1993 (LOST TO: Dan Kroffat)
4. 23/08/1993 (DEFEATED: Dan Kroffat) - 12/07/1994 (LOST TO: Dan Kroffat)
5. 30/06/1996 (DEFEATED: Yoshinari Ogawa) - 24/07/1996 (LOST TO: Tsuyoshi Kikuchi)

- Combined days as champion: 2,443
- Combined defences: 24

4. Joe Malenko

Joe's father, The Great Boris Malenko, had been a major figure in wrestling through the sixties and seventies, particularly in the Florida and Texas territories with experience of both All and New Japan. On retirement, Boris opened a training school in Florida, with his two sons, Joe and Dean, as assistant trainers and star pupils. Joe's first experience with Japan was with the UWF in May 1985, perfectly suited to his mat based, technical style, he gained experience battling Nobuhiko Takada and Yoshiaki Fujiwara among others in the short lived, ground breaking promotion.

He returned to Japan in February 1988 with his brother Dean, working as The Malenko Brothers, they were a formidable unit, earning universal plaudits for their stoic mat prowess. Earning a pin-fall victory over then World Jr. Heavyweight Champion Masanobu Fuchi in a tag match on 13th January 1989, Malenko challenged him one week later and shocked those attending in Fukuoka by bringing Fuchi´s two year reign to an end. However, just five days later, Malenko himself was defeated, losing the title and returning to tag contests for the rest of the tour.

When Malenko next retuned in July, the AJPW World Jr. Champion was Mitsuo Momota, son of Rikidōzan and a veteran who had battled Joe´s father sixteen years previously in 1973. Joe challenged directly and outclassed the older man, becoming champion for the second time, holding the belt until October when Masanobu Fuchi got his win and his title back. Joe Malenko toured extensively with All Japan until 1992, making further Japanese excursions with NJPW and the UWF-I before retiring in 2010 following one final run with AJPW as part of the Real World Tag League.

REIGNS

1. 20/01/1989 (DEFEATED: Masanobu Fuchi) - 25/01/1989 (LOST TO: Mighty Inoue)
2. 01/07/1989 (DEFEATED: Mitsuo Momota) - 20/10/1989 (LOST TO: Masanobu Fuchi)

- Combined days as champion: 116
- Combined defences: 2

CLASSIC MATCH N°1

Date: 11th July 1989
Location: Nakajima Sports Centre, Sapporo
Attendance: 3,800

JOE MALENKO vs DEAN MALENKO

Brothers of a thousand holds. Joe subdues Dean with a cravate as The Malenko Brothers clash in a catch-as-catch-can classic over the AJPW World Jr. Heavyweight Championship.

5. Mighty Inoue

Debuting in 1967, Inoue was a bruising technician who began his career with International Wrestling Enterprise. Benefiting greatly from the IWE´s working relationship with the AWA, Inoue became a star in the seventies with wars against Ric Flair, Nick Bockwinkle and Verne Gagne, winning the IWA World Heavyweight Title in 1974.

As IWE and All Japan began to cooperate in the mid-70s, Inoue made regular appearances on joint shows and in AJPW tournaments, capturing the All Asia Tag Team Titles alongside Animal Hamiguchi on one such occasion in 1977. When IWE closed its doors, Inoue moved full time to AJPW, working as a heavyweight and in the tag team division he won the All Asia Tag Titles once more, this time with Ashura Hara in 1983, a year which also saw him unsuccessfully challenge Chavo Guerrero for the NWA International Jr. Heavyweight Championship. The feud with Guerrero spilt into the following year and finally saw Inoue capture the title in late February and he would go on to have the longest reign, standing at 468 days, until Dynamite Kid finally deposed him in Summer 1985.

Remaining focused on the tag team division, becoming a multiple time champion, Inoue would not challenge for a junior title until his tag feud with The Malenko Brothers afforded him the opportunity in January 1989. Unable to beat the Malenkos, no matter who he chose as a partner, it was a surprise when Inoue toppled Joe Malenko to become AJPW World Jr. Heavyweight Champion. Inoue gave a good showing of himself as champion, with two successful defences in as many months, before dropping the title in March to Masanobu Fuchi. It would be a last hurrah, Inoue would never again hold or challenge for a major title, officially retiring on the night of AJPW´s 25th Anniversary in May 1998.

REIGNS
1. 25/01/1989 (DEFEATED: Joe Malenko) - 08/03/1989 (LOST TO: Masanobu Fuchi)
Combined days as champion: 42
Combined defences: 2

6. Shinichi Nakano

A product of the New Japan dojo, Shinichi Nakano debuted in March 1980 with a defeat to Hiro Saito. Toiling on the undercard, Nakano was still in the opening match slot when Riki Choshu broke away from NJPW to form JPW and invade All Japan; joining those departing, Nakano saw the chance to improve his standing. Unfortunately, this did not quite come to pass, with Nakano more often than not on the wrong end of the pin-fall with future hardcore icon Tarzan Goto and Mitsuo Momoto the only men he would regularly defeat until his luck started to change in 1987.

In October he battled Masanobu Fuchi to a double count out when challenging for the AJPW World Jr. Heavyweight Championship and in November he partnered Tiger Mask (Misawa) in the Real World Tag League, the association with Tiger Mask especially helping to boost Nakano´s stature going into 1988. Partnering Shunji Takano, Shinichi Nakano enjoyed a brief run in September as All Asia Tag Team Champion and once more challenged Masanobu Fuchi, though on this occasion he lost the match clean. The third time the pair meet over the title, in the Korakuen Hall, April 1989, Nakano was triumphant, finally winning the Junior Heavyweight Championship and rising to the top of the division.

Sadly, this reign lasted just four days, the shortest in the title´s history, as he was defeated by Momota almost as soon as he had won the title. One more unsuccessful attempt to defeat Fuchi for the championship followed in 1990, before Nakano left All Japan, spending time in SWS, WING and WAR before retiring where he had begun, with New Japan in 2001.

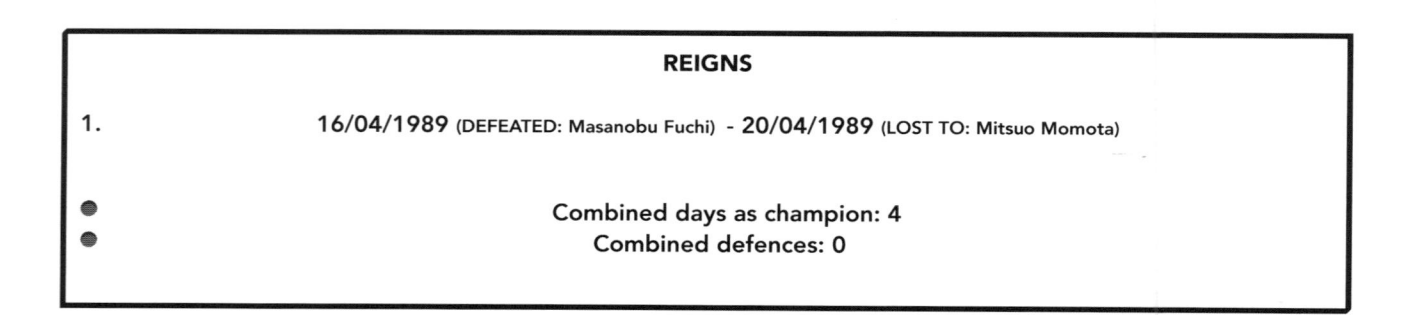

REIGNS
1.　　　　16/04/1989 (DEFEATED: Masanobu Fuchi) - 20/04/1989 (LOST TO: Mitsuo Momota)
Combined days as champion: 4 Combined defences: 0

7. Mitsuo Momota

Son of Rikidōzan, Mitsuo Momota debuted for his father's JWA promotion in 1970, but when his trainer, Giant Baba, left the following year Momota joined him in the fledgling All Japan Pro-Wrestling. Winning the second ever match in All Japan history, this proved something of a false dawn as Momota was still paying his dues and would only receive a notable push in 1976 following time spent in Mexico and Texas.

Although his matches were routinely first or second on the card, Momota went undefeated for most of the following decade, beating the likes of Onita and Fuchi and then Misawa and Kawada, helping them learn their craft. And this was very much Momota's role in the coming years, a dependable technical wrestler without his father's need for the limelight, Momota helped build the foundations for the careers of countless young wrestlers.

This role within the company meant that Momota never challenged for a major title, until the 25th of February 1989, when, at the age of 41, he got his first title match, a losing effort to fellow veteran Mighty Inoue, challenging for the AJPW World Jr. Heavyweight Championship. Staying in contention, Momota next unsuccessfully challenged Masanobu Fuchi, before finally succeeding, capturing his first title in March by nipping the reign of Shinichi Nakano in the bud. A two-month reign of his own followed, with two successful defences, before Joe Malenko reclaimed the title and relegated Momota back down the card.

A lengthy in-ring career followed, continuing to wrestle into his seventies, Momota grew into a much respected figure behind the scenes as the years passed, working as co-vice president of AJPW and vice president of NOAH until Misawa's death in 2009.

REIGNS
1. 20/04/1989 (DEFEATED: Shinichi Nakano) - 01/07/1989 (LOST TO: Joe Malenko)
• Combined days as champion: 72
• Combined defences: 2

8. Dan Kroffat

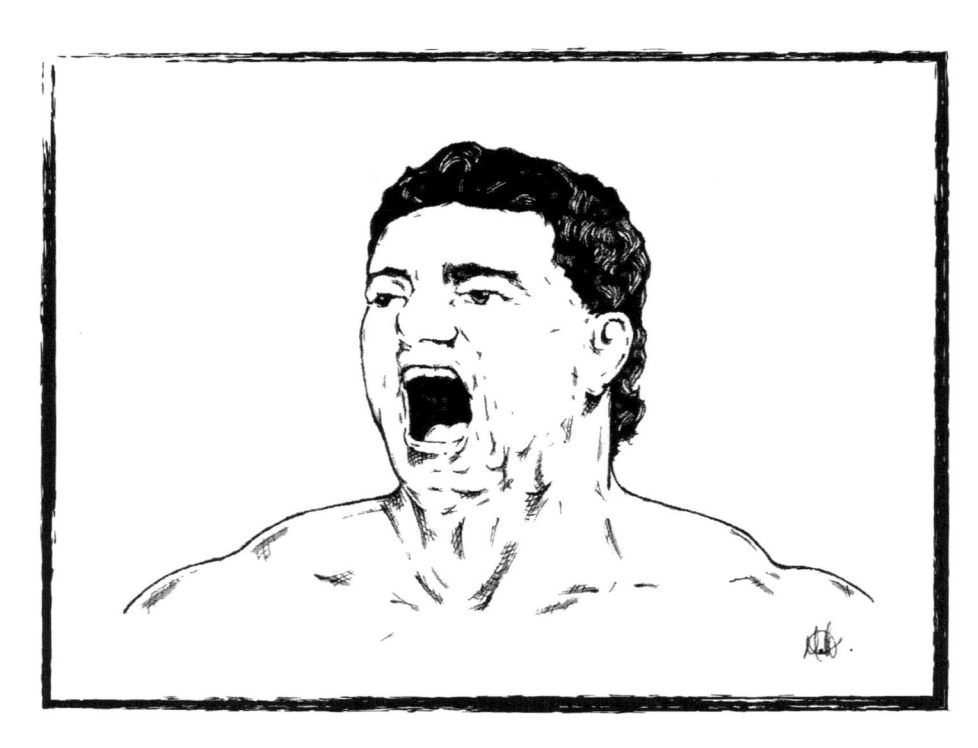

A product of the Hart Dungeon, the Ontario native, Philip Lafond debuted for Stampede Wrestling in June 1983 under the name Phil Lafon. His first exposure to Japan came just over a year later, spending October 1984 with the UWF where he battled Akira Maeda and Yoshiaki Fujiwara among others, acquitting himself well and laying foundations that would be vital for him in years to come.

After a number of years back in Canada, both with Stampede and the Montreal based International Wrestling, where Lafond first wrestled as Dan Kroffat, he returned to Japan for AJPW in October 1988. Part of a clique of foreign wrestlers, Kroffat appeared in tag matches alongside Danny Spivey and Tom Zenk before finding his ideal partner in Doug Furnas, the two going on to have countless classic matches and five indomitable All Asia Tag Team Championship reigns as the Can-Am Express. Their tag dominance limited the opportunities provided for singles championship glory, though one such occasion came in May 1993 which Kroffat seized by defeating Masanobu Fuchi, winning the AJPW World Jr. Heavyweight Championship and bringing Fuchi's three and a half year reign to an end. It was not long before Fuchi won the belt back at his first opportunity in August, but it had further established Kroffat as a top tier international competitor.

By the end of 1993, Kroffat and Furnas were tag champions again, belts they held for over a year, and simultaneously Kroffat continued to chase Fuchi, beating him once more for the Junior Championship in July 1994, making him a double champion. Main-eventing in tag contests against Misawa and Kobashi whilst defending his junior title against the best of a new generation, from Rob Van Dam to Yoshinari Ogawa, Kroffat was among the very top wrestlers in the world at this time. Eventually, the tag belts were lost to the Holy Demon Army and the junior title to Ogawa, with the Can-Am Express staying with AJPW until 1997 when they moved to the WWF, leaving a legacy of greatness in All Japan.

REIGNS
1.   21/05/1993 (DEFEATED: Masanobu Fuchi) - 23/08/1993 (LOST TO: Masanobu Fuchi)
2.   12/07/1994 (DEFEATED: Masanobu Fuchi) - 10/09/1995 (LOST TO: Yoshinari Ogawa)
Combined days as champion: 519
Combined defences: 6

9. Yoshinari Ogawa

Graduating from the AJPW Dojo under Giant Baba, Ogawa debuted for All Japan in September 1985 aged 18, losing each match on the undercard until the graduation of the next batch of trainees. A turning point came in 1987, when Ogawa joined Tenryu´s group Revolution, tagging with fellow members Fuyuki and Kawada in mid and occasionally upper-card bouts with Tenryu over the next three years.

On Revolution´s disbanding, Ogawa joined Tsuruta-gun, again rising up the card in multi man matches. It was as a member of Tsuruta-gun that Ogawa received his first title opportunity, alongside fellow member Masanobu Fuchi, an unsuccessful challenge in July 1992 for the All Asia Tag Team Championships and October of the same year saw Ogawa fail to topple Fuchi for the Junior Heavyweight Championship.

It would be September 1994, now as a member of the Holy Demon Army, when Ogawa next challenged for the Junior Title, losing to Dan Kroffat in the first of a three-match series that would stretch to September 1995, when Ogawa finally overcame the dominant Canadian to win the title for the first time. The centrepiece of the Junior division, a lengthy reign followed for Ogawa, until his forebear Fuchi reclaimed the belt for one final run in June 1996; another long run with the belt followed for Ogawa in 1997 until he was beaten by Maunakea Mossman. When Mossman vacated the title in 1998 to ascend to the heavyweight division, a tournament was held to determine a new champion, with Ogawa defeating all put in his path to become Junior Heavyweight Champion once more in July 1998.

Becoming part of The Untouchables alongside Misawa and Kakihara, Ogawa more than lived up to the moniker, winning the All Asia and AJPW Tag Titles in 1999, all the while defending his junior heavyweight title. Dependable and resilient in the mould of Masanobu Fuchi before him, Ogawa held the championship for two years before vacating it to join Misawa in NOAH.

REIGNS

1. **10/09/1995** (DEFEATED: Dan Kroffat) - **30/06/1996** (LOST TO: Masanobu Fuchi)
2. **15/01/1997** (DEFEATED: Tsuyoshi Kikuchi) - **22/08/1997** (LOST TO: Maunakea Mossman)
3. **19/07/1998** (DEFEATED: Satoru Asako) - **16/06/2000** (Vacated on leaving the company)

- Combined days as champion: 1,211
- Combined defences: 10

10. Tsuyoshi Kikuchi

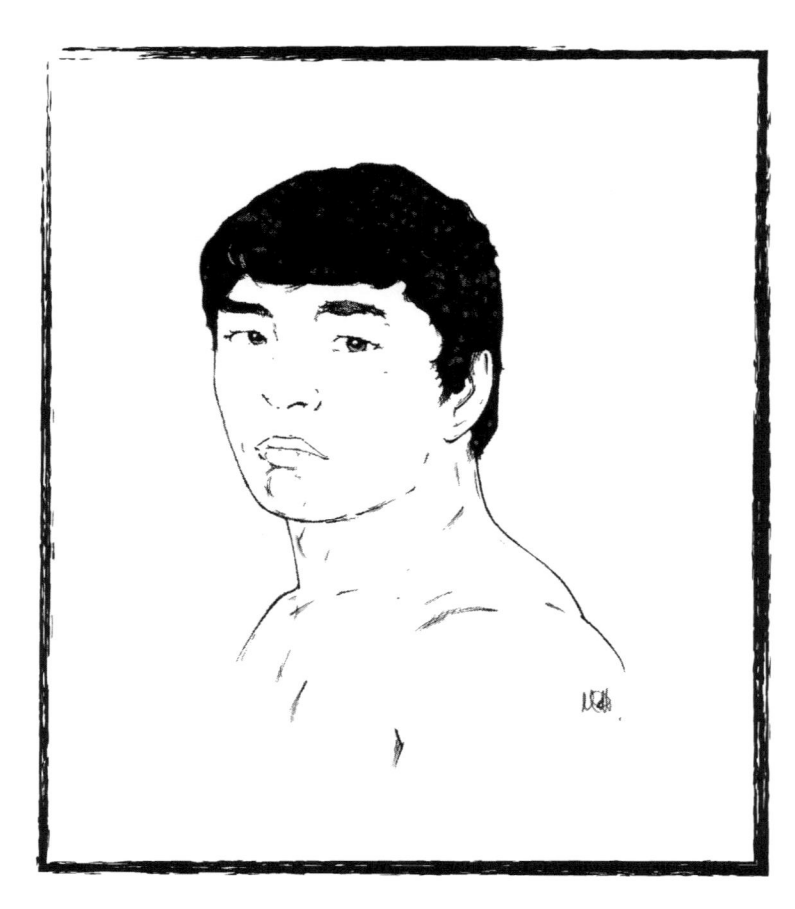

Tsuyoshi Kikuchi debuted from the AJPW dojo on the 26th of February 1988 in a losing effort to Mitsuo Momota, a match he would repeat 59 times in his debut year alone. Following a traditional trajectory in his early years, it was tag-team competition that helped him rise in stature; battling the Can-Am Express alongside first Tiger Mask and then Joe Malenko, helped show the handsome Kikuchi in a positive light and it was not long after that he became a member of the Super Generation Army.

Feuding with Tsuruta-gun allowed Kikuchi multiple opportunities to challenge Masanobu Fuchi for the World Jr. Heavyweight Championship, but he was unsuccessful on five separate occasions between 1990 and 1993; Kikuchi would, instead, find great success in the tag division alongside Kenta Kobashi, with the pair holding the All Asia Tag Team Championship for over a year between 1992 and 1993.

In 1995 Kikuchi switched allegiances to the Holy Demon Army and was a key figure in the early days of the stable, rejecting Kobashi, Misawa and Akiyama and main eventing as part of epic faction battles. With the Holy Demon Army in ascendancy heading into 1996, Kikuchi first challenged Ogawa unsuccessfully in March for the AJPW World Jr. Championship before a strong run of victories through the year led to him successfully challenging Fuchi in July to become champion.

Holding the title into the new year, with defences over Satoru Asako and Rob Van Dam, this was Kikuchi´s only singles championship in AJPW, relieved of the belt by Ogawa in January 1997, he promptly returned to undercard matches unless wrestling alongside other members of the Holy Demon Army. Kikuchi would only challenge for the Jr. Championship once more, in early 2000, before departing at the birth of NOAH later in the year.

REIGNS
1. 24/07/1996 (DEFEATED: Masanobu Fuchi) - 15/01/1997 (LOST TO: Yoshinari Ogawa)
Combined days as champion: 175
Combined defences: 2

11. Maunakea Mossman

Nephew of the legendary Curtis Iaukea, a massive brawler who had been a star for the NWA in his native Hawaii, before woking for the WWF and then All Japan throughout the seventies, Maunakea Mossman was the Hawaiian State amateur wrestling champion while still a high-schooler. On his graduation and on the recommendation of his uncle, Giant Baba invited Maunakea to the All Japan dojo from which he graduated on the 26th November 1994 in defeat to Kentaro Shiga. Enduring the traditional hard going in his early years, Mossmen´s first title opportunity came in July 1996 when he partnered Rob Van Dam in a losing effort, facing Akiyama and Omori for the All Asia Tag Team Titles.

Tagging with the biggest names in All Japan, such as Kobashi, Hansen and Misawa, Mossman was positioned as a contender for singles success relatively quickly, defeating Yoshinari Ogawa for the AJPW World Jr. Heavyweight Title at his first attempt in August 1997. A month later Mossman represented AJPW alongside Kobashi, defeating Hayabusa and Jinsei Shinzaki in FMW, showing that he was seen as a man with the brightest of futures in AJPW.

A dominant Junior Heavyweight Champion, Mossman held the title until vacating it in June 1998 to pursue further glory as a heavyweight.

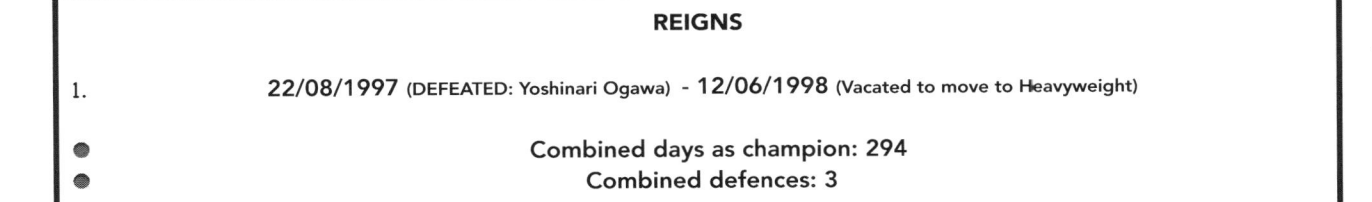

REIGNS

1. 22/08/1997 (DEFEATED: Yoshinari Ogawa) - 12/06/1998 (Vacated to move to Heavyweight)

Combined days as champion: 294
Combined defences: 3

12. Kendo Kashin

Kashin´s last match in New Japan had been a successful defence of the IWGP Jr. Heavyweight Championship, undefeated, he vacated the title to follow Keiji Muto to All Japan, instantly establishing himself as a top contender to the AJPW version of the title he had left behind.

There had not been a World Jr. Heavyweight Champion in All Japan since June 2000, when Ogawa left it behind to join NOAH and so a decision match was booked between the long term standard bearer Masanobu Fuchi and the new submission ace, Kashin. On submitting Fuchi on April the 13th 2002 Kashin became champion and held the belt for a staggering two years, defending it against the most diverse array of opponents from Gran Naniwa via The Great Sasuke to Dr. Wagner Jr.; Dr. Wagner would be his final defence in October 2003. Requiring time away, Kashin did not wrestle for All Japan again until March the following year, being stripped of the title in February due to his inactivity.

Kashin´s final match for All Japan at this time was on 12th of June 2004 in which he won the AJPW World Tag Team Titles alongside Yuji Nagata, titles which had to be vacated days later as, in what was becoming typical fashion, Kashin left the company to go freelance.

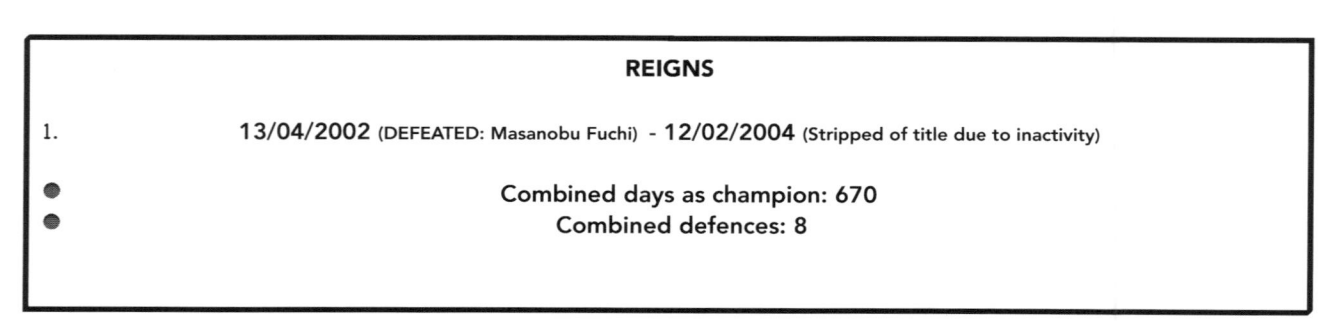

REIGNS
1.   **13/04/2002** (DEFEATED: Masanobu Fuchi) - **12/02/2004** (Stripped of title due to inactivity)
Combined days as champion: 670
Combined defences: 8

13. Kaz Hayashi

Trained by Gran Hamada, Hayashi debuted under a mask and the name Shiryu for UWF in January 1993, before joining Michinoku Pro at the peak of the promotion´s power. Whilst a Michi-Pro talent, Hayashi was able to work with WAR and NJPW, become a founding member of Kaientai and challenge The Great Sasuke for the IWGP Jr. Heavyweight Title. 1998 saw Hayashi participate in that year´s Best of the Super Juniors for NJPW before signing full time with WCW, removing his mask and wrestling as Kaz Hayashi. Despite the fame Hayashi found as a member of the high flying Jung Dragons, championships eluded him in the United States, but his time there brought him into close contact with Keiji Muto and the two formed a friendship that would heavily influence the rest of Hayashi´s career.

On returning to Japan in 2002, Hayashi started working with AJPW following its rebirth under Muto´s management, spending much of his first year reunited with his trainer Gran Hamada and former team mate Jimmy Yang before a burst of success in 2004. Teaming with Satoshi Kojima, working as both themselves and their alter egos (Kojima became the Great Kosuke and Hayashi reverted to Shiryu) the pair won the AJPW World and All Asia Tag Team Titles. Following Kashin being stripped of the World Jr. Heavyweight Championship, Hayashi battled TAKA Michinoku and won to become a triple champion, embarking on a reign mostly centred around a feud with Kaientai Dojo. In September 2004, Hayashi battled Hi69 in a match where both his Junior Heavyweight and Hi69´s STRONGEST-K Titles were on the line, Hayashi won and spent the rest of the year defending both titles across AJPW and Kaientai Dojo shows. The feud culminated in, and Hayashi´s reign ended as TAKA Michinoku took both championships in January 2005 on a K-Dojo event in the Korakuen Hall. 2005 also saw Hayashi participate in NOAH for the first time and it would be a NOAH invader, Naomichi Marufuji from whom he would next win the Junior Heavyweight Championship in early 2009.

What followed was a spectacular two year reign, sensationally seeing him reach the final of the 2009 Champion Carnival and defend the belt 17 times, the most for any single reign. It would eventually be Minoru Tanaka to take the belt, with Hayashi staying the staunchest of hero figures for All Japan, until following Keiji Muto away from the company with the formation of WRESTLE-1.

REIGNS

1. 22/02/2004 (DEFEATED: Blue-K) - 10/01/2005 (LOST TO: Taka Michinoku)
2. 06/02/2009 (DEFEATED: Naomichi Marufuji) - 02/01/2011 (LOST TO: Minoru)

- Combined days as champion: 1,018
- Combined defences: 23

14. TAKA Michinoku

Trained by Gran Hamada and The Great Sasuke, Takao Yoshida debuted age 18 in 1992 as TAKA Michinoku, adopting the name Michinoku as a sign of respect for The Great Sasuke. Michinoku Pro was where TAKA made his name, alongside Sasuke and Super Delfin, flying higher and moving faster than anyone else at the time. This led to appearances in New Japan, FMW (where he won the Independent World Jr. Heavyweight Title) and eventually the WWF.

Winning the new WWF Light Heavyweight Championship live on pay-per-view in 1997 catapulted Michinoku to a stratospheric level of fame as wrestling entered a new boom period in the USA and he spent much of the following five years in the States. The intensive schedule and the gradual defining down of Michinoku´s status in the company over time led him to return to Japan at the end of 2001 to recuperate and start afresh.

Establishing his own promotion, Kaientai Dojo, TAKA began to work tirelessly as a freelancer, making his first appearance in AJPW in May 2003, teaming with Muto to defeat Kojima and The Great Sasuke. He would begin to make more frequent All Japan appearances toward the end of the year, participating in the Real World Tag League and joining the faction RO&D, consisting of former WWE super stars. Losing to Hayashi in a match for the vacant World Jr. Heavyweight Championship, sparked a year long feud that saw K-Dojo stars appear on AJPW shows and Hayashi winning the STRONGEST-K Title leading to a match in January 2005 where Hayashi put both belts on the line, which Michinoku won.

Over the following ten months Michinoku wrestled for AJPW, K-Dojo, DDT Pro, NOAH, Dragon Gate and Apache Pro, managing to defend the title 12 times in this short period of time. Eventually he was overwhelmed by his schedule, losing the title to Shuji Kondo, challenging for the title only once more when it was held by Kaz Hayashi in 2010.

REIGNS
1. 10/01/2005 (DEFEATED: Kaz Hayashi) - 22/10/2005 (LOST TO: Shuji Kondo)
Combined days as champion: 285
Combined defences: 12

15. Shuji Kondo

Following his departure from Dragon Gate, the muscle bound powerhouse, Shuji Kondo debuted for AJPW alongside YASSHI and TARU in March 2005. With cohesive support from his long time friend YASSHI, the imposing Kondo became one half of the All Asia Tag Team Champions within three months of his arrival; the pair becoming founding members of one of pro-wrestling´s most enduring factions, Voodoo Murders, in September.

Voodoo Murders´ feud with RO&D set Kondo up to challenge RO&D member TAKA Michinoku on the 22nd October 2005 for the AJPW World Jr. Heavyweight Championship, a match which Kondo won, starting a year and a half reign of dominance. Voodoo Murders propagated a reign of terror during this time, appearing as a unit in both New Japan and NOAH in addition to All Japan, making a host of enemies as they did so.

February 2007 saw Shuji Kondo and TARU defeated by the powerful student/teacher tandem of Nakajima and Sasaki, establishing Nakajima as the challenger who would end Kondo´s first reign. Beginning to tag more with Suwama and Kaz Hayashi, Kondo found himself at odds with Voodoo Murders as time went by, eventually leaving the group and coming to stand for all that was good in AJPW, staying in constant contention for championship gold. It was in the guise of AJPW representative that Kondo went to NOAH and defeated Yoshinobu Kanemaru for the GHC Jr. Heavyweight title in September 2012 and then went on to defeat Hiroshi Yamoto in January 2013 for the AJPW Jr. Championship to become double champion. Yoshinobu Kanemaru would have his revenge though, returning to All Japan to defeat Kondo and end his second reign.

Later in the year, Muto established a new company, WRESTLE-1, which Kondo joined and it was where he spent much of his time, though he would return sporadically throughout 2018 as a WRESTLE-1 representative, winning the World Jr. Heavyweight Championship on one such occasion, losing it two months later to Koji Iwamoto.

REIGNS
1. 22/10/2005 (DEFEATED: TAKA Michinoku) - 17/02/2007 (LOST TO: Katsuhiko Nakajima)
2. 02/01/2013 (DEFEATED: Hiroshi Yamato) - 23/02/2013 (LOST TO: Yoshinobu Kanemaru)
3. 22/09/2018 (DEFEATED: Koji Iwamoto) - 29/11/2018 (LOST TO: Koji Iwamoto)
• Combined days as champion: 603
• Combined defences: 6

16. Katsuhiko Nakajima

The prodigious Nakajima made his first appearance for All Japan aged just 16, a day after he had wrestled Jushin Thunder Liger in the Tokyo Dome for NJPW in May 2004. Balancing his career between All and New Japan, whilst appearing for a wide range of promotions vying for his services Nakajima´s first title was claimed in AJPW.

Winning the All Asia Tag Team Championship alongside his mentor Kensuke Sasaki in July 2005, Nakajima soon became a double champion by winning the World Jr. Light Heavyweight Title in ZERO-1. Utilising his speed, lightning strikes and suplexes, Nakajima held both titles deep into 2006, a year in which he reached the finals of the AJPW Jr. Heavyweight League and began to feud intently with Voodoo Murders, specifically the AJPW World Jr. Heavyweight Champion Shuji Kondo.

In January 2007 Nakajima defeated Kondo´s cohort YASSHI to become number one contender and in due course overcame the Voodoo Murders´ numbers game to defeat Shuji Konndo in February and take his Jr. Heavyweight Championship. Nakajima held the belt for a year, defending against Voodoo Murders´ members for the most part without difficulty, though this changed in the later half of the year and the addition of new member Silver King. The legendary luchador seemed to have the youngster´s number, securing a number of tag victories over him and pushing him to the limit the first time he challenged for the belt, the match being declared a no contest as a result of a fractured bone in Nakajima´s hand. On his return in 2008, Silver King defeated Nakajima to claim the title, with Nakajima making his move to NOAH later in the year.

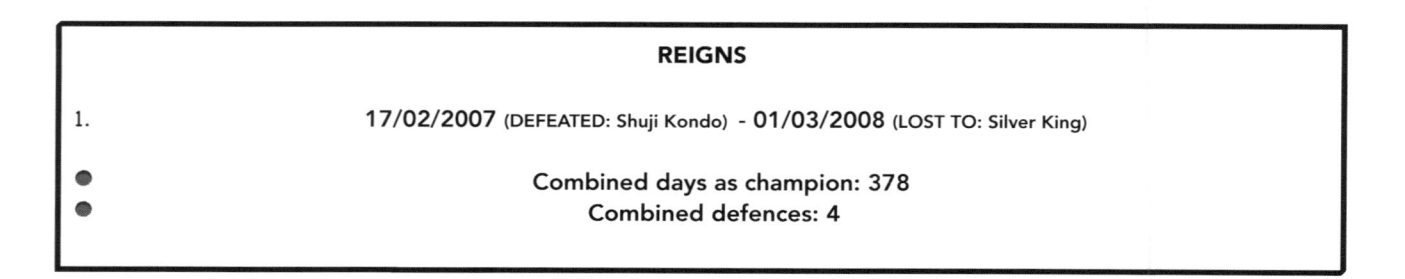

REIGNS
1.   17/02/2007 (DEFEATED: Shuji Kondo) - 01/03/2008 (LOST TO: Silver King)
Combined days as champion: 378
Combined defences: 4

17. Silver King

Son and student of the legendary luchador Dr. Wagner, César González debuted in 1985 under the name El Invasor, before quickly adopting his mask and the character of Silver King. Working on a regular basis in Mexico for UWA, it was not long before Silver King´s first trip to Japan, touring with AJPW as Dr. Wagner Jr., throughout October 1987, before returning to Mexico and losing his mask in a lucha de apuesta against El Hijo de Santo.

Throughout the 90s Silver King worked primarily for the UWA and then CMLL winning numerous singles and tag championships before a two year spell with WCW, but returned to Japan sporadically to tour with WING and the IWA. Following his departure from WCW and rejoining CMLL, he started touring regularly with NJPW, first as Silver King, often tagging with his brother (who had adopted the Dr. Wagner Jr. moniker) and then under the guise of Black Tiger III.

It would be 2004 when Silver King returned to AJPW, a tour in march that saw he and his brother win 6 matches in 7 nights before unsuccessfully challenging Kojima and Hayashi for the All Asia Tag Championships. Returning alone in September 2007, Silver King associated himself with the wicked Voodoo Murders stable and went undefeated to earn the right to challenge Nakajima for the World Jr. Heavyweight Championship. Due to an injury to Nakajima, the match was called off whilst in progress, with Silver King retaining his status as top contender; when the two next met in February 2008 Silver King emerged triumphantly as the new champion. Holding the belt for two months, Silver King lost to Ryuji Hijikata in his first defence, making his last appearance for AJPW in August 2008, losing to KAI in the finals of the Junior Heavyweight League before returning to Mexico.

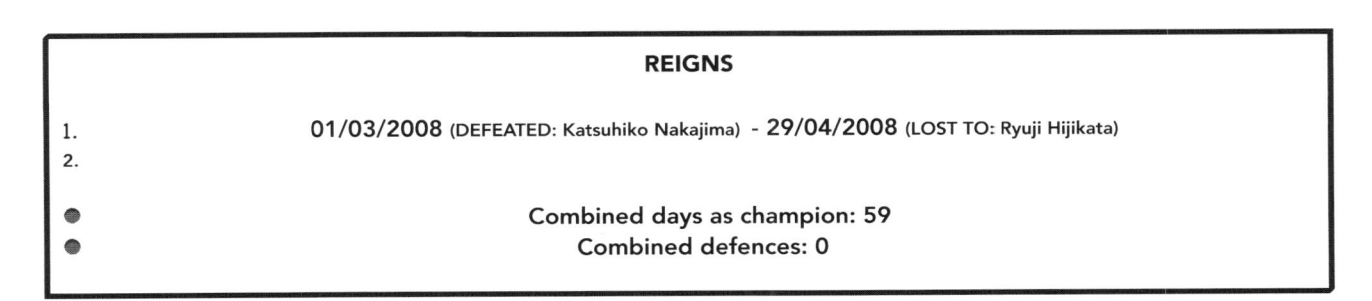

REIGNS

1. 01/03/2008 (DEFEATED: Katsuhiko Nakajima) - 29/04/2008 (LOST TO: Ryuji Hijikata)
2.

- Combined days as champion: 59
- Combined defences: 0

18. Ryuji Hijikata

Student of famed grappler Yuki Ishikawa, Hijikata transitioned seamlessly from a high school judo background into the shoot-style environment of Ishikawa´s Battlarts promotion, debuting in 1998. On the losing end of most bouts across Battlarts, FMW and Michinoku Pro, Hijikata was in the midst of the traditionally tough learning process for a pro-wrestler when he debuted for All Japan in July 2000, committing himself full time to the company the following year.

Though a proficient grappler, results were still very much mixed for Hjikata, he challenged Kendo Kashin for the AJPW World Jr. Heavyweight Championship in July 2003, but was defeated in under ten minutes and rarely rose above the undercard.

Things began to change in early 2005 as Hijikata adopted a mask and the new name Toshizo, catching crowd imagination and experiencing a run of victories hitherto unknown to Hijikata, leading to him challenging TAKA Michinoku for the Junior Heavyweight Championship in June. Voluntarily unmasking as a show of respect to TAKA following his defeat, that same respect was now seen towards Hijikata as he experienced a significant boost in popularity whilst battling the factions of Voodoo Murders and RO&D.

In 2008, alongside Katsuhiko Nakajima, he won the AJPW Jr. Tag League and less than a month later he rode this momentum to victory over Silver King, becoming World Jr. Heavyweight Champion. Defences followed against Kaz Hayashi, El Samurai and KAI before the invader Naomichi Marufuji unseated Hijikata in September. Hijikata would switch from hero to villain soon after his title loss, joining Voodoo Murders under his Toshizo persona and he would remain in the group until leaving AJPW to go freelance in June 2010.

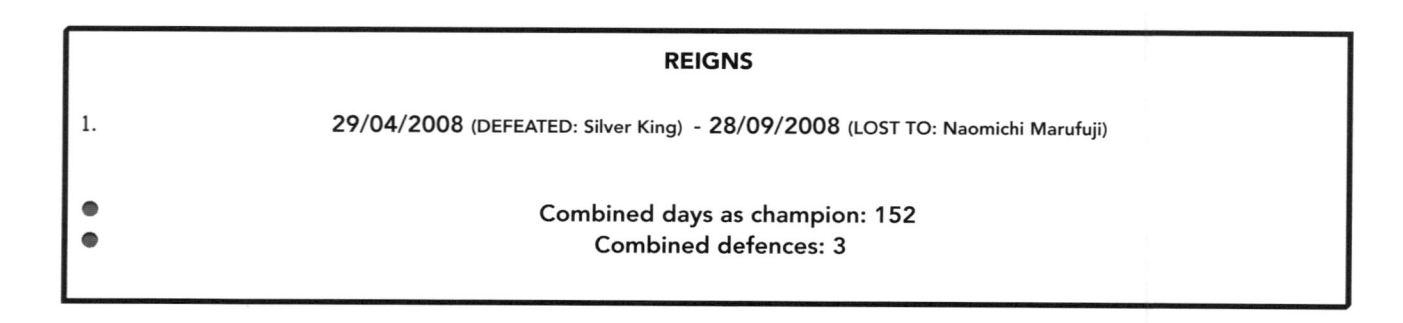

REIGNS
1. 29/04/2008 (DEFEATED: Silver King) - 28/09/2008 (LOST TO: Naomichi Marufuji)
Combined days as champion: 152
Combined defences: 3

19. Naomichi Marufuji

As a product of the All Japan dojo and as Mitsuharu Misawa´s protege, Marufuji had debuted for AJPW in 1998 in a losing effort to Yoshinobu Kanemaru. In his last few matches in All Japan in mid-2000 Marufuji began to be given room to show flashes of his spectacular brilliance in tag matches alongside his mentor Misawa, but it was only through leaving AJPW for NOAH that Marufuji became the sensation that he did.

Marufuji did not set foot in an All Japan ring from the moment NOAH was established until September 2008, in the interim he had won every title available in NOAH and, in the process, become an international superstar. Shockingly, Marufuji strode into AJPW on the 28th of September 2008 and directly defeated then Junior Heavyweight Champion Ryuji Hijikata, winning the title and returning with it to NOAH.

Marufuji defended the title more times in a NOAH ring than in AJPW, his first defence being a double title bout for both the GHC and AJPW Jr. Heavyweight Championships against his eternal rival KENTA which went to a sixty-minute time limit draw. Further defences followed against NOSAWA and veteran Kikuchi with Marufuji only appearing twice more in All Japan; the first time in a match of the year against the sublime Shuji Kondo and the second in defeat to AJPW hero Kaz Hayashi.

Debuting for AJPW in 1998, returning 10 years later to win the World Jr. Heavyweight Championship, Marfuji returned once more in 2018 to win the Champion Carnival to scratch his ten-year itch whilst remaining fully committed to his position as vice-president of NOAH.

REIGNS

1. 28/09/2008 (DEFEATED: Ryuji Hijikata) - 06/02/2009 (LOST TO: Kaz Hayashi)

Combined days as champion: 131
Combined defences: 4

20. Minoru

On leaving NJPW in January 2009, having spent the preceding decade at the forefront of the IWGP Jr. Heavyweight division, Minoru landed directly in All Japan the following month. Aligned with Voodoo Murders, Minoru was seen as an instant contender to the World Jr. Heavyweight Championship, wrestling a near forty-minute technical masterpiece with Kaz Hayashi in a losing effort for the title in March.

Remaining a prominent figure within Voodoo Murders, Minoru worked high profile tag matches with fellow members and reached the semifinals of both the 2009 and 2010 Junior Heavyweight Leagues. His next shot at the title came following his victory in a six-man ladder match to claim n°1 contender status in November 2010 with the title match set for January. Nearly two years earlier Minoru had been Hayashi´s first challenger for the World Jr. Heavyweight Championship and he would also be his seventeenth and last, Minoru ending Hayashi´s spectacular second reign.

Minoru himself, held the belt until June 2011, defending it once against Shuji Kondo, but found himself involved in controversy which led to his suspension and his being stripped of the title. Leader of Voodoo Murders, TARU, was involved in a fight with fellow member Mitsu Hirai backstage, leading to Hirai suffering a stroke. Among measures taken as punishment for the incident Voodoo Murders was disbanded and all Japanese members suspended for failing to intervene. Minoru´s suspension was lifted by the end of the month and he returned to action for AJPW, where he remained until joining WRESTLE-1 in 2013.

REIGNS
1. 02/01/2011 (DEFEATED: Kaz Hayashi) - 03/06/2011 (Vacated due to suspension)
Combined days as champion: 152
Combined defences: 1

21. KAI

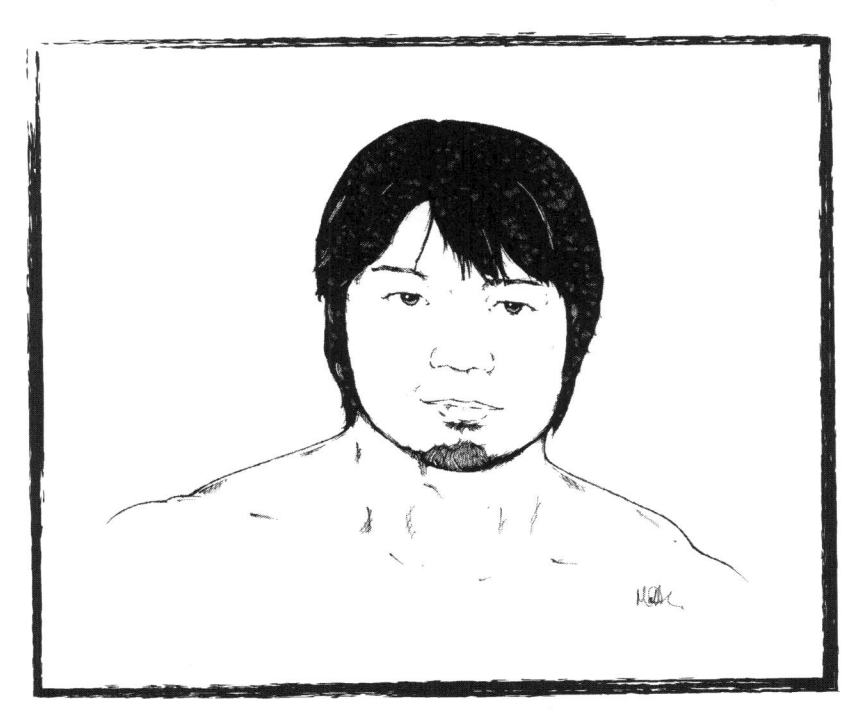

Having received initial training from Animal Hamaguchi, Atsushi Sakai entered further tutelage from Kaz Hayashi and Keiji Muto, making his debut as part of his preparation for AJPW in Mexico in early 2007 under the name Kai.

One year later, All Japan recalled Sakai to Japan, capitalised his name and gave him a successful debut as KAI in a tag battle alongside Hiroshi Yamato. His success would continue into his debut year, winning the Junior Heavyweight League and being part of new group, F4, alongside his friend Yamato and Satoshi Kojima, feuding with Voodoo Murders and Minoru Suzuki´s GURENTAI.

Titles initially eluded KAI, but this changed in 2011, catalysed by his partnering with his trainer Hayashi at the start of the year. The pair succeeded in winning the Junior Tag League, defeating the team of the Junior Heavyweight Champion Minoru and Koji Kanemoto to do so. The two then faced off to decide who would challenge Minoru, with KAI emerging victorious in May, but Minoru was suspended and the belt vacated before the challenge could take place. It was decided that Shuji Kondo would be KAI´s opponent for the vacant title in a match which took place on the 19th June 2011, which KAI won to become champion for the first time.

On his return from suspension, Minoru was KAI´s first challenger, but Kai´s momentum swept him to victory and also led to him winning the 2011 Jr. Heavyweight and Real World Tag Leagues (the latter alongside Seiya Sanada). His standout year was spoiled in October by the invasion of DDT-Pro talent, Kenny Omega, who defeated him for the World Jr. Heavyweight Championship, but in May 2012 KAI gained revenge and recaptured the title from Omega in the main event in front of a sold out Korakuen Hall. The second reign was ended by long term ally Hiroshi Yamato in August, with KAI declaring two weeks later that he would take a break to prepare his body for a transition to the heavyweight division.

REIGNS

1. 19/06/2011 (DEFEATED: Shuji Kondo) - 23/10/2011 (LOST TO: Kenny Omega)
2. 27/05/2012 (DEFEATED: Kenny Omega) - 12/08/2012 (LOST TO: Hiroshi Yamato)

- Combined days as champion: 203
- Combined defences: 2

22. Kenny Omega

By 2011 Kenny Omega had been a regular DDT-Pro performer for three years and had established himself as among the very top tier of wrestlers active in Japan, having won both the KO-D and IWGP Jr. Heavyweight Tag Titles alongside Kota Ibushi.

2011 saw DDT-Pro enter into a working relationship with AJPW and, as a result, Kenny Omega participated in that year's Junior Heavyweight League. Although he did not win the tournament, among the matches he won was his first match, which was against the reigning AJPW World Jr. Heavyweight Champion and eventual tournament winner, KAI. As Omega had been the only one to beat KAI during the tournament, he was granted a title opportunity in October and capitalised emphatically, claiming victory and returning to DDT-Pro with the AJPW Jr. Heavyweight Championship.

Omega´s reign was dazzling, defending the belt five times, including a classic with Shuji Kondo in April 2012, displaying prime athletic ability combined with brash villainous stylings making him the perfect antagonist in front of AJPW crowds. KAI eventually got his return match in May and succeeded in reclaiming his title, with Omega retuning to AJPW only once more, to unsuccessfully challenge Hiroshi Yamato for the title he had lost in October 2012. After which Kenny continued his story with DDT-Pro, before jumping full time to NJPW.

REIGNS

1. 23/10/2011 (DEFEATED: KAI) - 27/05/2012 (LOST TO: KAI)
   Combined days as champion: 217
   Combined defences: 5

23. Hiroshi Yamato

Following a near identical introduction to pro-wrestling as KAI, Hiroshi Yamato passed from the stewardship of Animal Hamaguchi to that of AJPW and Keiji Muto, making his debut in Mexico as part of his learning process.

Both Yamato and KAI returned together establishing a team and eventually a faction alongside Satoshi Kojima and Aaron Aguilera, battling Voodoo Murders. Whilst his contemporary KAI enjoyed a modicum of individual success in his early years with All Japan, this was not so much the case with Yamato, who often lost decisively in his singles encounters and struggled for the spotlight alongside Kojima and KAI. February 2010 saw an opportunity for Yamato to be his own man as the stable F4 was forced to disband following defeat to Voodoo Murders, yet Yamato swiftly formed another tag team, this time with Shuji Kondo. Reaching the finals of the 2010 Junior Tag League and challenging for the All Asia tag titles in July, the pair experienced moderate success, though Yamato´s momentum was halted with a defeat to KAI which eliminated him from the 2010 Junior Heavyweight League.

When KAI won the World Jr. Heavyweight Championship in June 2011, Yamato split from Shuji Kondo and set his sights on overcoming his long term friend and rival, challenging him first, unsuccessfully, in August 2011. 2012 would finally be Yamato´s year to emerge from the shadows. In July he won the Junior Hyper League, defeating legend Koji Kanemoto and former partner Kondo in the same night to win the semi-final and final respectively.

This victory gave Yamato the right to once more challenge KAI in August 2012, this time successfully claiming the World Jr. Heavyweight Championship. Holding the title until the new year, Yamato successfully defended it five times, overcoming Kaz Hayashi and Kenny Omega among others before losing the title to Shuji Kondo in a match where both the GHC and AJPW titles were on the line in January 2013. In the following months, Yamato won the All Asia Tag Team titles alongside Hikaru Sato, before leaving AJPW in September to join the newly formed WRESTLE-1.

REIGNS
1. 12/08/2012 (DEFEATED: KAI) - 02/01/2013 (LOST TO: Shuji Kondo)
Combined days as champion: 143
Combined defences: 5

24. Yoshinobu Kanemaru

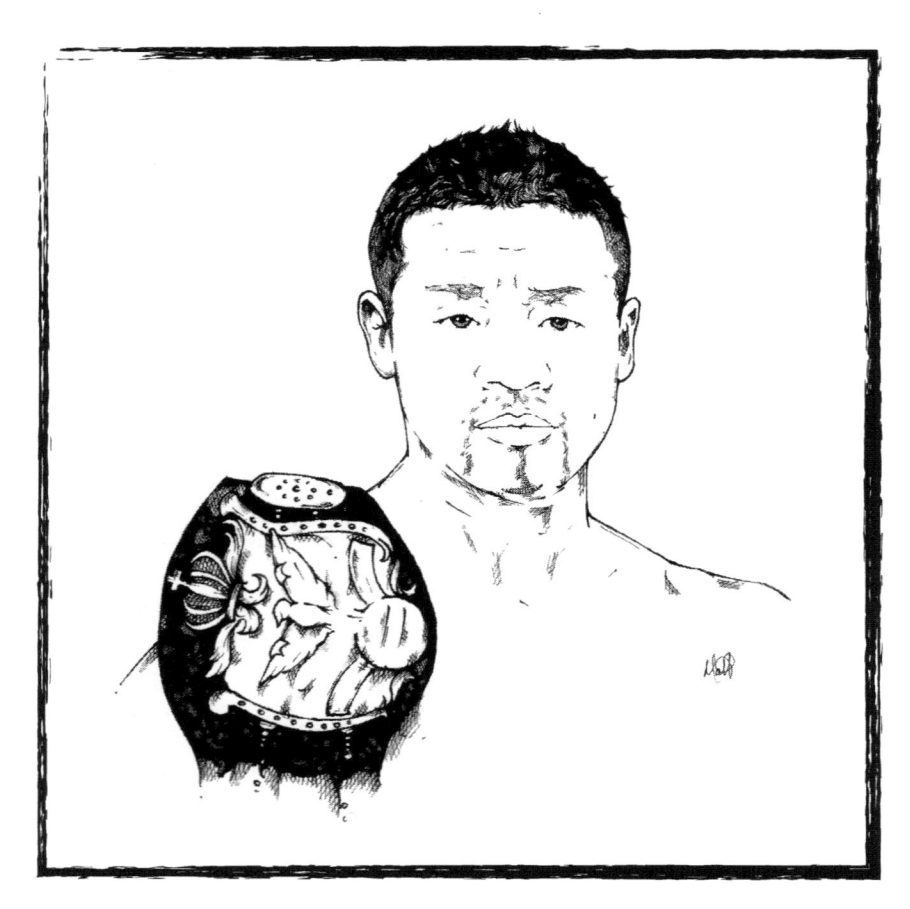

Having debuted for All Japan in 1996, a dependable, technical junior heavyweight, Kanemaru had never once so much as challenged for a title during his original four year tenure with the company. Despite this, Kanemaru´s status was greatly enhanced by his recruitment into Kenta Kobashi´s Burning stable, with whom he served as their junior member between 1998 and 2000 before the exodus to NOAH.

During 13 years with NOAH, Kanemaru had grown into a junior heavyweight ace, a true ring general, oozing character and wisdom and in January 2013 he returned to AJPW. The circumstances were those of protest as he and fellow original Burning member, Jun Akiyama, and a number of others left NOAH outraged at the manner in which Kenta Kobashi had been dismissed by those in charge at NOAH at that time. These former NOAH talents established Burning in AJPW once more and were instantly recognised as top championship contenders, with Kanemaru winning the AJPW World Junior Heavyweight Championship from Shuji Kondo in his first singles match since returning.

Kanemaru held the belt for the rest of the year as Burning dominated both the junior and tag divisions for the entirety of 2013, with his reign being ended by the newly arrived Último Dragón. Two more years with All Japan followed in which Kanemaru added to his legend by winning the All Asia Tag Championships twice (once with Akiyama and once with Último Dragón), before returning to NOAH and joining Suzuki-gun.

REIGNS

1. 23/02/2013 (DEFEATED: Shuji Kondo) - 15/12/2013 (LOST TO: Último Dragón)

Combined days as champion: 295
Combined defences: 7

25. Último Dragón

Since returning to wrestling in 2002 following surgery in 1998 which had caused him severe nerve damage, Último Dragón enjoyed the status of a wandering legend. Among the myriad organisations Último Dragón worked with, he appeared in special attraction tag team matches for AJPW in 2003, 2008 and 2011 before beginning to wrestle for All Japan on a more regular basis from 2013 onward.

His first match in All Japan for two years came in September 2013 as he battled representatives of Burning, including the AJPW World Jr. Heavyweight Champion Yoshinobu Kanemaru in a tag contest, ending in a loss for Último Dragón. Dragón returned on the 8th of December and gained revenge, with his team of luchadores gaining victory over Burning in a six-man tag, leading to his challenging Kanemaru for the Junior Title one week later in the Korakuen Hall. The two veterans battled for twenty minutes on AJPW Fan Appreciation Day 2013, with the hero Último Dragón winning the championship to send the crowd home happy.

Entering the new year as champion, Último Dragón defended his title against former members of Burning Atsushi Aoki, and Kotaro Suzuki, succumbing finally in May to the second challenge of Aoki. Dragón would win the title once more in August 2017 in a late Summer feud with fellow veteran Tajiri, claiming the title from him on the 27th of the month before losing it two months later in October. Último Dragón continues to work a busy schedule, lending the wisdom gained from his years in the ring to his opponents and delighting crowds eager to see a legend at work.

REIGNS
1. 15/12/2013 (DEFEATED: Yoshinobu Kanemaru) - 25/05/2014 (LOST TO: Atsushi Aoki)
2. 27/08/2017 (DEFEATED: Tajiri) - 21/10/2017 (LOST TO: Tajiri)
• Combined days as champion: 220
• Combined defences: 3

26. Atsushi Aoki

A national championship winning amateur wrestler, Atsushi Aoki graduated from the NOAH dojo on Christmas Eve 2005, facing legends Misawa and Taue in a tag match alongside fellow debutant Yoshinori (Ippei) Ota. From that highest of highs, Aoki began the new year at the bottom rung of the ladder, enduring early challenges, yet growing in confidence, stature and ability though exposure to a wide range of national and international opponents and a learning excursion to Europe. In 2009 Aoki participated in NJPW's Best of the Super Juniors and Super J Cup tournaments, in both instances taking losses to Prince Devitt. This, in turn, lead to Aoki challenging Devitt unsuccessfully for the IWJP Jr. Heavyweight Championship in a bruising technical encounter in July 2010.

In February 2013 Aoki was part of the NOAH group joining AJPW to reform Burning and was placed in instant contention for the All Asia Tag Team titles alongside Kotaro Suzuki. Although the pair were unsuccessful in their initial challenge, the following month they won the Junior Hyper Tag League and became champions at the second try at the end of April 2013. Aoki successfully challenged Último Dragón for the Jr. Heavyweight Championship in May, setting in motion a lengthy reign consisting of five defences and ten months. It was his former partner, Kotaro Suzuki, who brought it to an end, but when Suzuki left AJPW the belt was vacated, necessitating a tournament, which Aoki won to become champion again in February 2016.

By this time, Aoki had been appointed head of talent relations, appearing over the coming years in DDT-Pro, FMW and BJW as a proud ambassador for his company. Two All Asia Tag Title reigns with Hikaru Sato followed as did a third, six-month reign as the Junior Heavyweight Champion in 2018 before Aoki won the belt for the last time from Koji Iwamoto in May 2019. Just two weeks later, Atsushi Aoki tragically died in a motorcycle accident leaving the company and the industry shocked and broken hearted with AJPW decreeing that he be recognised as World Jr. Heavyweight Champion until 20th of November 2019. At the time of his passing, Aoki had continued in his role as President of Talent Relations and was also the head trainer at the AJPW dojo, a much loved kindly man whose absence will be felt for many years to come.

REIGNS

1. 29/05/2014 (DEFEATED: Último Dragón) - 27/03/2015 (LOST TO: Kotaro Suzuki)
2. 21/02/2016 (DEFEATED: Hikaru Sato) - 19/06/2016 (LOST TO: Hikaru Sato)
3. 03/02/2018 (DEFEATED: Tajiri) - 26/08/2018 (LOST TO: Koji Iwamoto)
4. 20/05/2019 (DEFEATED: Koji Iwamoto) - 20/11/2019 (Vacated)

- Combined days as champion: 807
- Combined defences: 12

CLASSIC MATCH N°2

Date: 14th December 2014
Location: Korakuen Hall, Tokyo
Attendance: 1,111

ATSUSHI AOKI vs MASANOBU FUCHI

Those who tend the flame burn brightest and for the longest time. Two guardians of AJPW tradition from very different generations clash as Masanobu Fuchi chases his sixth reign and pushes Atsushi Aoki to his limit for twenty thrilling minutes.

27. Kotaro Suzuki

Having left NOAH to join All Japan in February 2013 as part of the Burning stable, Kotaro Suzuki did not have to wait long for his first championship opportunity. Teaming with Atsushi Aoki, the two chased the All Asia Tag Team Titles, held on their arrival in the company by junior heavyweight icons Koji Kanemoto and Minoru Tanaka.

Winning the Junior Tag League, Suzuki and Aoki challenged for and won the Tag Championships on the 25th April 2013. Holding the titles for the rest of the year, this was in parallel to Suzuki's Burning team mate, Yoshinobu Kanemaru's success as he had similarly won he World Jr. Heavyweight Championship soon after arriving from NOAH. In order to challenge Kanemaru, Suzuki broke away from Burning in November 2013, but lost his title match held at the end of the month. 2014 started well for Suzuki, winning the Junior Battle of Glory, he earned the right to challenge Último Dragón, though was once more unsuccessful in his attempt to become Junior Heavyweight Champion. Despite this, 2014 did see him win the GAORA TV Championship and the All Asia Tag Team Titles once more, this time beside Kento Miyahara.

2015 started in similar fashion, winning the 2015 Junior Battle of Glory by beating his former team mate and reigning Junior Heavyweight Champion Atsushi Aoki in the final. One month later Suzuki dethroned Aoki and began a lengthy reign of his own, lasting until November 2015 when, following contract disputes, Suzuki left All Japan to go freelance, vacating the title in the process.

REIGNS

1. 27/03/2015 (DEFEATED: Atsushi Aoki) - 16/11/2015 (LOST TO: Vacated on leaving the company)

Combined days as champion: 234
Combined defences: 6

28. Hikaru Sato

Trained by Minoru Suzuki for both pro-wrestling and MMA, Sato started in Suzuki´s Pancrase Hybrid Wrestling Organisation in early 2000. An excellent mat based fighter, Sato complemented his grappling ability with gimmicks to help him stand out, such as walking to his fights in maid outfits. Such affectations lent Sato naturally to pro-wrestling and he started to transition over in 2008, making his debut for DDT Pro by knocking out the giant Shuji Ishikawa in May of that year.

Sato would remain affiliated with DDT-Pro for the rest of his career while working with a wide range of independent companies as a freelancer, beginning to make tournament appearances for All Japan in 2010. Sato made more regular appearances in AJPW from 2012 onward, a year which saw his first challenge for an AJPW title as he unsuccessfully battled his regular team mate Hiroshi Yamato in September for the AJPW World Jr. Heavyweight Championship. The two would work together in January to win the All Asia Tag Team Championship for a short reign which further established Sato as a serious contender in the company. Later in the year he would join the stable Evolution, alongside Suwama, Joe Doering and Atsushi Aoki, helping Sato rise to the forefront of the junior division alongside stablemate Aoki.

The two fought each other over the World Jr. Heavyweight Championship in February 2016 following Kotaro Suzuki´s departure, with Aoki the victor; yet Sato challenged once more in June, winning the match to become champion for the first time. The pair also won the All Asia Tag Titles in July for Hikaru Sato to briefly reign as a double champion, before losing the Junior Title to DDT-Pro wrestler Soma Takao. Holding the tag titles until the end of the year, Sato and Aoki also won the 2016 Jr. Tag Battle of Glory, before losing the belts to the veteran team of Onita and Fuchi. In 2017 Sato reached the finals of the Jr. Battle of Glory, before successfully defeating Keisuke Ishii to become Junior Champion once more in April and he and Aoki regained the All Asia Tag belts in June for him to again reign as a double champion, albeit briefly. Continuing to work primarily for AJPW, Sato is the rarest of men who perfectly balances his eccentric sense of humour with pristine grappling skill.

REIGNS

1. 19/06/2016 (DEFEATED: Atsushi Aoki) - 28/08/2016 (LOST TO: Soma Takao)
2. 28/04/2017 (DEFEATED: Keisuke Ishii) - 30/07/2017 (LOST TO: Tajiri)

Combined days as champion: 163
Combined defences: 5

29. Soma Takao

An independent pro-wrestler in high school, competing in hobbyist federations in Tokyo, Takao enrolled in the DDT-Pro dojo in 2009 and debuted in August of the same year.

A highly promising young talent, Takao won the Young Drama Cup in 2010 and looked set to achieve great things in the company. He challenged for the KO-D Openweight Title in 2011 and went on to win the KO-D Tag Team Championships alongside company founder Sanshiro Takagi in 2012 before founding the group Team Dream Futures with Keisuke Ishii and Shigehiro Irie in 2013. Team Dream Futures went about invading other promotions as the brash face of the DDt-Pro youth movement, one such promotion was AJPW for whom Takao had his first match on November 2013.

The group participated in AJPW's single and tag tournaments in 2014 and even brought the KO-D six man Tag Championship with them, defending it on an All Japan show in August. The following year saw the group sporadically appearing in AJPW, antagonising veteran wrestlers while lighting a fire under AJPW's own younger figures like Jake Lee and Kento Miyahara. It would be in a clash with veteran Hikaru Sato, on the biggest DDT-Pro show of the year, Ryogoku Peter Pan 2016, that Soma Takao sensationally won the AJPW World Jr. Heavyweight Championship and found himself at the forefront of AJPW's own youth revolution. Takao defended the title successfully once on a DDT-Pro show in September, before returning to AJPW and losing it to one time Team Dream Futures partner Keisuke Ishii in November. Takao returned to AJPW in 2018 to participate in the Junior Battle of Glory, but has since focused his energy on his home promotion, DDT-Pro.

REIGNS
1. 28/08/2016 (DEFEATED: Hikaru Sato) - 27/11/2016 (LOST TO: Keisuke Ishii)
Combined days as champion: 91
Combined defences: 1

30. Keisuke Ishii

In 2007, Keisuke Ishii attended an open audition to be considered for the AJPW dojo but, despite passing the audition itself, Ishii was not selected to join and he instead enrolled in that of DDT-Pro, making his debut for the company in July 2008.

Winning the 2009 Young Drama Cup, the first winner of the trophy, Ishii challenged for the KO-D Openweight Title the following year and was the jewel in the crown of DDT-Pro's youth movement. In late 2010, Ishii made his first appearance in NJPW, defeating Hiromu Takahashi, a young man whose path would cross Ishii's on a number of occasions though 2011 in New Japan prior to Ishii forming a regular tag team with Shigehiro Irie as the foundation of Team Dream Futures in DDT-Pro. Team Dream Futures first invaded All Japan in September 2013 with Ishii and Irie defeating the team of Atsushi Aoki and Kazushi Miyamoto, going on to challenge Burning for the All Asia Tag Team Championship in October. Dividing their time between DDT-Pro and All Japan throughout 2014, Ishii and Irie won the All Asia Tag Titles by defeating Akiyama and Kanemaru on a DDT-Pro Show in April, holding the belts until August.

Ishii first challenged for the AJPW World Jr. Heavyweight Title in May 2015, losing to Kotaro Suzuki, but remaining a frequent visitor to All Japan as Team Dream Futures continued to function as a dominant tag unit. This continued until June 2016 when the team fell apart and member Soma Takao won the AJPW World Jr. Heavyweight Championship, starting to feud with Ishii in DDT-Pro. This feud spilt over into All Japan as Ishii challenged Takao successfully for the title, becoming champion for the first time and ruining Takao's first defence.

Ishii defended the title across both DDT-Pro and All Japan, participating as champion in the 2017 Junior Battle of Glory, holding the belt until he was defeated by Hikaru Sato in April of that year in his final AJPW match to date before returning to DDT-Pro.

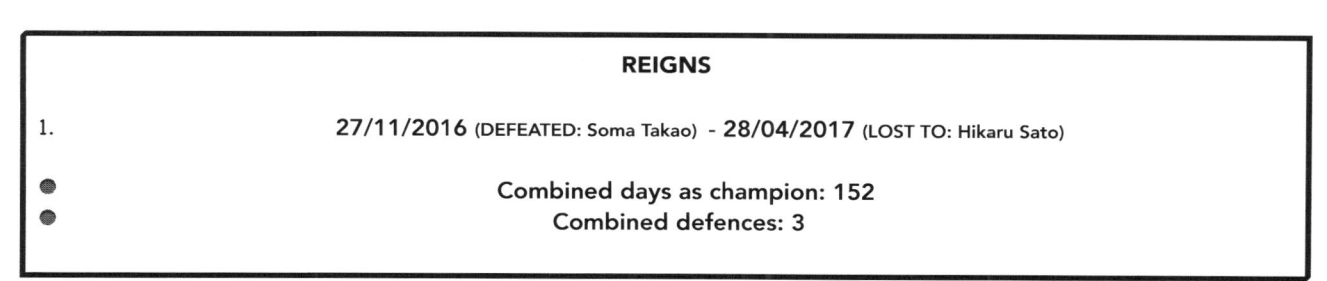

REIGNS

1. 27/11/2016 (DEFEATED: Soma Takao) - 28/04/2017 (LOST TO: Hikaru Sato)

Combined days as champion: 152
Combined defences: 3

31. Tajiri

With a kickboxing background yet enamoured with Mexican wrestling, Yoshihiro Tajiri enrolled in Animal Hamaguchi's gym from which he graduated in September 1994, debuting for IWA Japan. In his first year of wrestling Tajiri also debuted for BJW and was invited to the USA where he challenged Dan Severn for the NWA World Heavyweight Title, a few months later travelling to Mexico to wrestle for CMLL. A spectacular aerialist with vicious kicks and a true business mind, Tajiri was destined from the start to travel wildly and achieve great things.

BJW became Tajiri's home promotion in his early years and he became their inaugural Junior Heavyweight Champion in 1998, a year in which he also appeared for New Japan and toured Mexico with CMLL before coming to rest in ECW. Staying with the company until its closure in 2001, ECW saw Tajiri evolve from a clean cut athlete into a highly marketable, mist spewing villain and his work there made him a highly bankable commodity for years to come. Five memorable years followed with the WWE, with Tajiri winning multiple championships, before he returned to Japan at the start of 2006 to work with the eccentric HUSTLE.

In his return year of 2006, Tajiri made his first appearance in AJPW, battling the Great Muta, though as these appearances grew more frequent in 2007 the two usually teamed together. Participating in the 2007 Champion Carnival, Tajiri unsuccessfully challenged Minoru Suzuki for the Triple Crown. Consummate freelancer, once HUSTLE had folded, Tajiri started his own companies, SMASH and WNC while appearing sporadically all over the Japanese wrestling scene, though neither company lasted long. In search of stability, Tajiri rekindled his relationship with Keiji Muto and spent two years devoted to WRESTLE-1 before returning on a regular basis to AJPW in July 2017. With legend status from the moment of his arrival, he challenged and defeated Hikaru Sato on July 30th to become AJPW World Jr. Heavyweight Champion for the first time, though he lost it on his first defence to fellow legend Último Dragón a month later. Staying in AJPW and staying focused on the title, Tajiri snatched it back from Dragón in October, this time holding it until February 2018. An irrepressible warrior and an invaluable asset, Tajiri continues to wander the wrestling landscape, with all doors open to him.

REIGNS

1. 30/07/2017 (DEFEATED: Hikaru Sato) - 27/08/2017 (LOST TO: Último Dragón)
2. 21/10/2017 (DEFEATED: Último Dragón) - 03/02/2018 (LOST TO: Atsushi Aoki)

- Combined days as champion: 133
- Combined defences: 3

32. Koji Iwamoto

Having been trained in Nagoya by local company, Sportiva Entertainment, Koji Iwamoto debuted at the end of 2012. Learning his craft over the following years primarily working for Heat Up Pro-Wrestling and DDT-Pro, Iwamoto also made appearances for WRESTLE-1 and Dragon Gate before starting to appear regularly for All Japan in 2016.

A rugged athlete with a strong amateur wrestling base to his ring work, Iwamoto first challenged for the AJPW World Jr. Heavyweight Championship in 2017 following an incident during that year's Junior Battle of Glory where his match with the reigning champion Keisuke Ishii ended in a double knockout. Unsuccessful on this occasion, Iwamoto mostly found himself battling members of Evolution, again unsuccessfully challenging for the Junior Championship when it was held by Hikaru Sato in June 2017.

2018 would prove to be Iwamoto's breakout year, starting by reaching the finals of the Junior Battle of Glory, before a loss to Shuji Kondo, and continuing in June with the formation of a dominant young stable with Jake Lee and Dylan James known as Sweeper. Iwamoto unsuccessfully challenged Aoki for the Junior Heavyweight belt in July, but swiftly earned a rematch and became World Jr. Heavyweight Champion for the first time in August. Despite dominating tag team competition with his new colleagues, this reign was short, ended by Shuji Kondo in September only for Iwamoto to claim the title back again in November. Iwamoto won the 2019 Junior Battle of Glory and became a double champion as he and Jake Lee won the All Asia Tag Team Titles in March, before Atsushi Aoki brought his Junior reign to an end in May. Iwamoto's future is undeniably a bright one and as long as he remains a junior heavyweight, he will be in permanent contention for the World Jr. Heavyweight Championship.

REIGNS

1. 26/08/2018 (DEFEATED: Atsushi Aoki) - 22/09/2018 (LOST TO: Shuji Kondo)
2. 29/11/2018 (DEFEATED: Shuji Kondo) - 20/05/2019 (LOST TO: Atsushi Aoki)
3. 25/07/2020 (DEFEATED: Susumu Yokosuka) - (CURRENT)

- Combined days as champion: 320+
- Combined defences: 5 +

33. Susumu Yokosuka

Trained by Ultimo Dragon, Susumu Mochizuki debuted in December 1998 for his teacher's Toryumon promotion in Mexico before returning to Japan to participate in the company's first ever event on Japanese soil in January 1999. Spending the following year bouncing between the two countries, the naturally charismatic Mochizuki gained a wealth of experience and stood out as a worthy contender in the thrilling new promotion.

The rise of Toryumon in Japan in 2000 coincided with a catastrophe for AJPW and Susumu Mochizuki was one of many outside wrestlers contracted to appear on All Japan shows at this time. He made his debut for the company in August 2000 and continued to appear sporadically over the following two years in high-octane multi man contests as part of the M2K faction. When the M2K group eventually dissolved, Susumu Mochizuki engaged in a match with Masaaki Mochizuki to determine who could retain their shared name. Susumu lost and adopted the name Yokosuka as a way of paying tribute to his home town.

As Mochizuki became Yokosuka and Toryumon became Dragon Gate, Susumu continued to build his reputation as a highly sympathetic team player. In addition to winning the company's top title in April 2006, he also became a multi-time Open the Twin and Triangle gate champion. Dragon Gate was Susumu Yokosuka's exclusive home for many years until he was announced as a surprise entrant into the tournament to crown a new World Junior Heavyweight Champion in late 2019. Dividing his time between All Japan and Dragon Gate, Yokosuka defeated the emotional favorite Hikaru Sato in the final to become AJPW's Junior Heavyweight Champion in January 2020.

Five sensational title defences followed, two of them before no fans as a result of the pandemic lockdown and one of them taking place in Dragon Gate, the first time the promotion had hosted the title. Yokosuka's final appearance in AJPW to date was on 25th July 2020 when he lost his championship to Koji Iwamoto, a loss which allowed him to return his focus to Dragon Gate and his fight to continue proudly flying the flag for Toryumon.

REIGNS

1. 03/01/2020 (DEFEATED: Hikaru Sato) - 25/07/2020 (LOST TO: Koji Iwamoto)

Combined days as champion: 204
Combined defences: 5

GHC JR. HEAVYWEIGHT CHAMPIONSHIP

Having first established its Heavyweight Championship via a tournament held in spring 2001, culminating in victory for company founder and icon Mitsuharu Misawa, the second GHC Championship which NOAH created was its Junior Heavyweight Championship. Following the successful format established in spring, a 12-man tournament was held between the 9th and 24th of June, 2001, the field primarily consisting of former All Japan Jr. Heavyweights looking for a fresh start, but also including Americans Matt Murphy and BJ Whitmer alongside luchadors Path Finder and Juventud Guerrera rounding out the group.

Juventud defeated Satoru Asako and Naomichi Marufuji to make it to the June 24th final and the man standing across from him before the bell rang was Yoshinobu Kanemaru. In the process of truly finding himself through the freedom afforded him by the advent of NOAH, Kanemaru had improved in leaps and bounds since following Misawa away from All Japan; this tournament seeing him overcome Path Finder and former All Japan World Jr. Heavyweight Champion Tsuyoshi Kikuchi to reach the final and the challenge of international star Juventud. Following a thrilling match in which the arrogant, but always brilliant Juventud dominated Kanemaru at times, Kanemaru battled back and won victory with a pair of brain busters followed by an emphatic moonsault press to win and become the first ever GHC Jr. Heavyweight Champion.

Kanemaru is a fine embodiment of the transformative power of NOAH and its GHC Jr. Heavyweight Championship. Those wrestlers who have won the title have never been content to work beneath the glass ceiling of weight or size restrictions. More than once the GHC Jr. Heavyweight Champion has risen to the status of top draw in the company, their junior title reign either being instrumental in their personal development before becoming heavyweights or their final goal, in itself the culmination of their journey.

1. Yoshinobu Kanemaru

A product of the AJPW dojo, primarily trained by Giant Baba, Kenta Kobashi and Jun Akiyama, Kanemaru debuted for AJPW at the age of 19 in July 1996. Although on the winning side of tag contests when paired with Kobashi and Misawa, it would be March 1998 before Kanemaru claimed a singles victory, over the debuting Makoto Hashi. Despite his talent, Kanemaru never challenged for the AJPW World Junior Heavyweight Championship and truly embraced the exodus to NOAH as a chance to spread his wings.

Changing his ring gear and incorporating more high flying moves into his hard hitting repertoire, Kanemaru moved quickly from being a utility player in All Japan to strong foundation of NOAH's junior division. Defeating Juventud Guerrera to become the first ever GHC Jr. Heavyweight Champion in June 2001, his second reign would also come about as a result of winning a tournament after the championship was vacated in spring 2002. During this reign, Kanemaru invaded NJPW alongside Tsuyoshi Kikuchi to claim the IWGP Jr. Tag Titles, an example of how foundations laid by Kanemaru helped those coming after him as the GHC Jr. Tag Titles were established in 2003 as a result of his success.

His third title reign lasted over a year and built perfectly to the high watermark for the division and a war with KENTA in front of 62,000 fans at the Tokyo Dome. He would have two more reigns last close to or over a year and seven in total, with each helping establish new challengers and new sides to his character, from the early years helping KENTA and Marufuji shine to helping establish Ishimori and Kotoge in his final years with NOAH. Few have done so much for a company or division as Kanemaru has for the GHC Junior division, having held the title twice longer than anyone else and defended it twice as many times, his position as all-time ace of the division is almost unassailable.

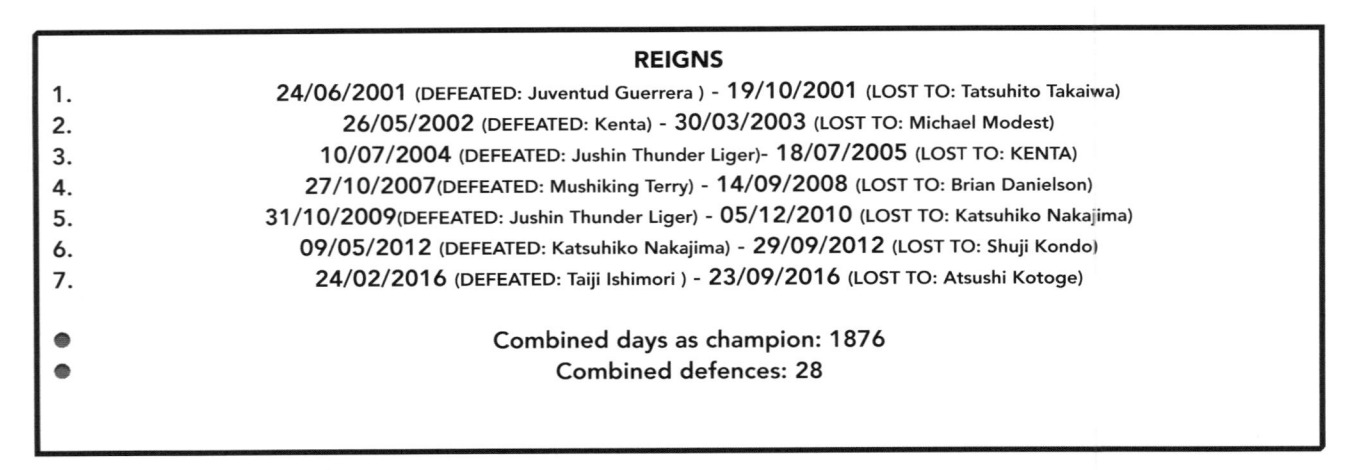

REIGNS

1. 24/06/2001 (DEFEATED: Juventud Guerrera) - 19/10/2001 (LOST TO: Tatsuhito Takaiwa)
2. 26/05/2002 (DEFEATED: Kenta) - 30/03/2003 (LOST TO: Michael Modest)
3. 10/07/2004 (DEFEATED: Jushin Thunder Liger) - 18/07/2005 (LOST TO: KENTA)
4. 27/10/2007 (DEFEATED: Mushiking Terry) - 14/09/2008 (LOST TO: Brian Danielson)
5. 31/10/2009 (DEFEATED: Jushin Thunder Liger) - 05/12/2010 (LOST TO: Katsuhiko Nakajima)
6. 09/05/2012 (DEFEATED: Katsuhiko Nakajima) - 29/09/2012 (LOST TO: Shuji Kondo)
7. 24/02/2016 (DEFEATED: Taiji Ishimori) - 23/09/2016 (LOST TO: Atsushi Kotoge)

- Combined days as champion: 1876
- Combined defences: 28

2. Tatsuhito Takaiwa

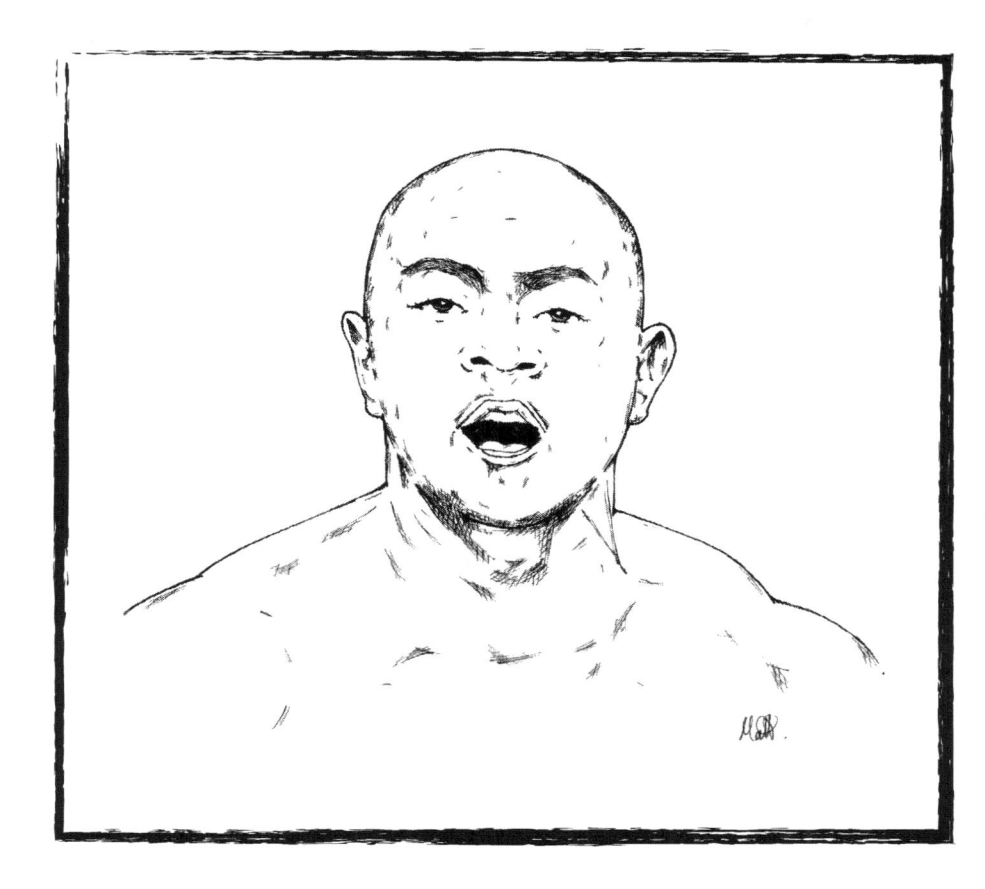

Following a highly successful 8 years with New Japan, Takaiwa moved to join his long term tag partner Shinjiro Otani in new promotion, ZERO-1, debuting for the company on its first show on the 2nd of March 2001.

Forming a tag team alongside Naohiro Hoshikawa in Battlarts, this pairing debuted for NOAH on the 26th of August 2001 against the team of Makoto Hashi and GHC Jr. Heavyweight Champion Yoshinobu Kanemaru, the veteran Takaiwa scoring the win for his team and in doing so foreshadowing a future challenge to Kanemaru. Following further tag matches between the two across ZERO-1 and NOAH in September, the challenge came in October, with Takaiwa earning a hard fought win and his first GHC Jr. Heavyweight Championship. Wrestling exclusively for NOAH whilst champion, it would be just two months until he was unseated by Marufuji and return to ZERO-1.

Takaiwa returned to unsuccessfully challenge Kanemaru in the Nippon Budokan in January 2005, but, with the exception of occasional tag team appearances, would not appear for NOAH again until the 23rd of December 2006. On this night, he once more challenged the GHC Jr. Heavyweight Champion, at this time Takashi Sugiura, and won the belt for the second time. During this reign he defended the title in ZERO-1, defeating the AWA World Jr. Champion to hold double gold in the process. However, come April and his next appearance in a NOAH ring, he lost his GHC title back to the spectacular NOAH talent Mushiking Terry (Kotaro Suzuki) before returning to ZERO-1 and forging on with his career as a veteran technician elevating the stature of every ring he graces with his presence.

REIGNS
1. 19/10/2001 (DEFEATED: Yoshinobu Kanemaru) - 09/12/2001 (LOST TO: Naomichi Marufuji)
2. 23/12/2006 (DEFEATED: Takashi Sugiura) - 28/04/2007 (LOST TO: Mushiking Terry)
• Combined days as champion: 177
• Combined defences: 3

3. Naomichi Marufuji

On graduating from the AJPW dojo in 1998, Naomichi Marufuji debuted in front of 1,500 people in the opening match of an All Japan house show, which he lost to Yoshinobu Kanemaru. Almost exactly two years later, in his final match for All Japan on a card dominated by heavyweights, he had progressed to the second match of the night, yet still lost to Yoshinobu Kanemaru. NOAH would truly set the young Marufuji free on their first show, appearing in the middle of the card, the junior heavyweights had twenty minutes to shine and nobody shone brighter than Marufuji, symbolically getting the win over Kanemaru.

In NOAH´s first year of business, Marufuji was built as a spectacular attraction, tagging with Misawa and appearing in other promotions, winning the WEW Tag Titles with Tamon Honda in FMW and stealing the show in defeat at the Nippon Budokan against Tatsuhito Takaiwa on ZERO-1´s second ever show in April 2001. Semifinalist in the tournament to crown the first ever GHC Jr. Heavyweight Champion, Marufuji would not have to wait too long before getting his first title shot.

On 9th December 2001, he challenged Takaiwa and gained revenge for his earlier loss to the veteran, winning the GHC Jr. Heavyweight Championship at his first attempt. However, what may very well have been a record setting title run was cut short on the seventh of April, when, during his second defence against Makoto Hashi, Marufuji incurred a serious knee injury, and, deeming him unable to continue, the referee awarded both the match and title to Hashi. Returning in 2003, Marufuji never held the GHC Jr. Heavyweight Championship again, going on instead to win every other title in NOAH, his short run with the Junior title setting him on the path to glory.

REIGNS
1. 09/12/2001 (DEFEATED: Tatsuhito Takaiwa) - 07/04/2002 (LOST TO: Makoto Hashi)
Combined days as champion: 119
Combined defences: 1

4. Makoto Hashi

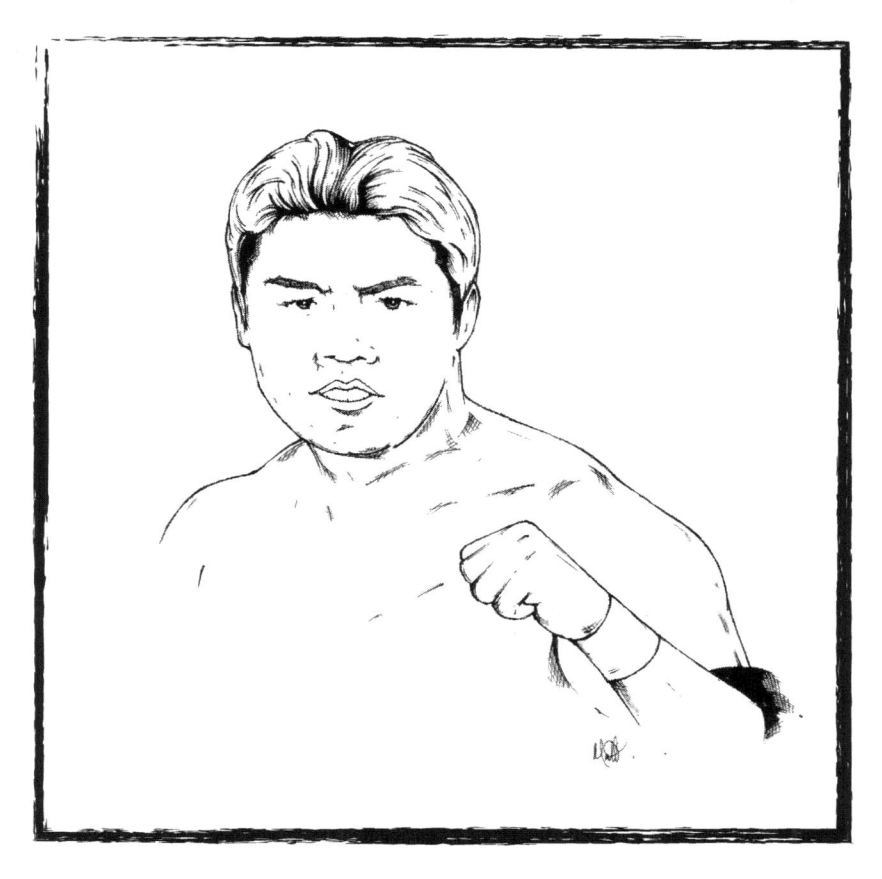

Graduating from the AJPW dojo in 1998, having primarily received training at the hands of Jun Akiyama, Makoto Hashi debuted with a loss to Yoshinobu Kanemaru on 25th of March 1998. Like many others of his weight division, despite his good looks and talent, in the years until the advent of NOAH, Makoto Hashi failed to progress beyond the second match on AJPW cards.

However, unlike a number of his contemporaries, Hashi continued to be outshone in the land of emerald green, NOAH´s debut show opened with Hashi enduring decisive defeat at the hands of Morishima. In the tournament to crown the inaugural GHC Jr. Heavyweight Champion Hashi suffered a second round exit to Marufuji and did very little of note to stand out from the roster in the subsequent months. In March 2002 he was on the winning side of a number of tag matches involving Marufuji to warrant challenging him for his Jr. Heavyweight Championship on 7th of April. After 20 minutes of action, the referee determined Marufuji unable to carry on, stopped the match and awarded Hashi the title. Far from gleefully accepting his opponents misfortune, Hashi vacated the title the following day, deeming his manner of victory dishonourable and a tournament to crown a new champion was set in motion.

Despite a sterling victory over Juventud Guerrera in the first round, the next round again saw Hashi´s exit, this time at the hands of eventual tournament winner and nemesis Yoshinobu Kanemaru. Makoto Hashi would unsuccessfully challenge for the GHC Jr. Heavyweight Championship only once more, before appearing in a classic tag match at the Tokyo Dome alongside his trainer Jun Akiyama against Marufuji and Minoru Suzuki in July 2005 and focusing his attention on the Hardcore Openweight Championship in the years to come.

REIGNS
1.   07/04/2002 (DEFEATED: Naomichi Marufuji) - 08/04/2002 (VACATED)
Combined days as champion: 1
Combined defences: 0

5. Michael Modest

A veteran of the California independent wrestling scene Mike Modest came to the attention of a much broader audience following the 2000 release of the seminal wrestling documentary Beyond the Mat in which his story played a featured role. Documenting his struggle to make it to the level of success that his ability deserved, he states on film that he would be best suited as a performer in Japan, where his style would be more respected and, following a brief spell under contract to WCW, it would be where he debuted with NOAH on 26th of August 2001.

With a powerhouse physique, Modest fit perfectly amongst NOAH's regular foreign legion at the time Scorpio, Vader, Bison Smith and Ron Harris, often wrestling in tag matches alongside his student, Donovan Morgan. His first title match for NOAH occurred on 24th November 2002, teaming with Morgan, they were unsuccessful in their attempt to dethrone the junior tag team champions Kikuchi and Kanemaru. Remaining a thorn in Kanemaru's side, Modest challenged for his GHC Jr. Heavyweight Championship in Fukuoka on 30th March 2003, and, on emerging victorious, became the first non-Japanese champion. Modest was also the first to successfully defend the title outside of Japan, putting it on the line during a brief return to California against Vito Thomaselli.

Following a loss to the tag-team of Takashi Sugiura and Yoshinobu Kanemaru, Sugiura was named Modest's next challenger, successfully defeating him for the title in September 2003. Modest remained a highly respected regular member of the NOAH roster until the end of 2005, when he returned to the USA.

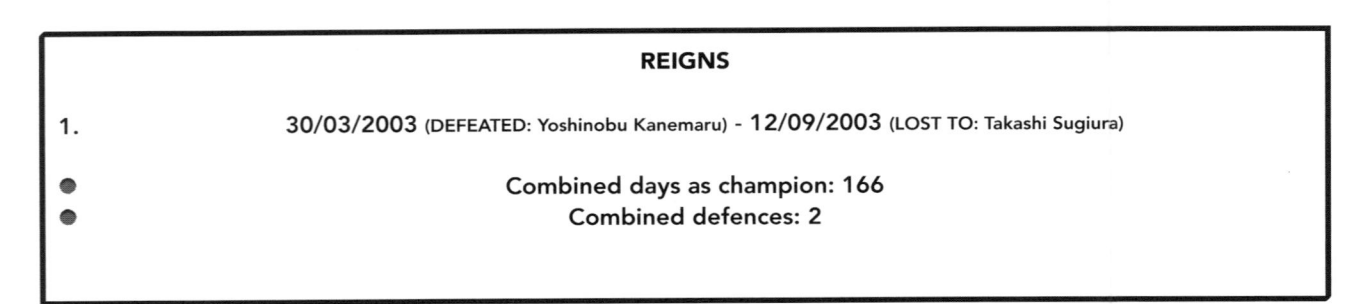

REIGNS
1. 30/03/2003 (DEFEATED: Yoshinobu Kanemaru) - 12/09/2003 (LOST TO: Takashi Sugiura)
• Combined days as champion: 166
• Combined defences: 2

6. Takashi Sugiura

The first man to make their pro-wrestling debut for NOAH, on 23rd December 2000, it was the Junior Heavyweight division in which Sugiura honed his craft. In keeping with tradition, for much of his first year as a wrestler, Sugiura was on the losing side of his in-ring battles, a powerful technician without the explosive violence of KENTA or graceful aerial skills of Marufuji, it would be his charisma and ability to tell a story between the ropes that saw him rise in stature.

In 2002 Sugiura unsuccessfully challenged for both the junior singles and tag team championships, both times defeated by Yoshinobu Kanemaru, these defeats prompting him to embrace Kanemaru as his partner and this relationship, either friendly as the pairing Sugi-Kane, or professional rivals over the years, greatly bolstered his rising popularity. As did a hugely successful run in New Japan´s Best of the Super Junior Tournament, 2003, which saw him reach the semifinals before losing to Koji Kanemoto; by September of the same year, when he defeated Mike Modest to become GHC Jr. Heavyweight Champion, he was seen as a major star rising to take his rightful place.

This first reign was entwined with New Japan, with his first defence against Gedo and culminating in a loss to Jushin Thunder Liger in the Tokyo Dome in January 2004. In the following years Sugiura experienced lengthy spells of success in the Junior tag team division, before winning a number one contender Battle Royale on 3rd June 2006 and successfully challenging KENTA for his Jr. Heavyweight Championship the following day. He would become a double champion on 13th August when he and Kanemaru were once more crowned Jr. Tag Team Champions, and stayed one until the return of veteran Tatsuhito Takaiwa who reclaimed the singles crown in December 2006. 2007 saw Sugiura turn heavyweight, a weight class he would come to dominate.

REIGNS

1. 12/09/2013 (DEFEATED: Michael Modest) - **04/01/2004** (LOST TO: Jushin Thunder Liger)
2. 04/06/2006 (DEFEATED: KENTA) - **23/12/2006** (LOST TO: Tatsuhito Takaiwa)

- Combined days as champion: 316
- Combined defences: 3

7. Jushin Thunder Liger

After one of the most successful decades in the career of any wrestler to ever step into a ring, Jushin Thunder Liger became invaluable as a standard bearer and a totem, a figure to elevate, not only junior heavyweight divisions, but entire companies.

First appearing in NOAH in 2002 as part of a junior tag team rivalry, helping to establish the GHC sanctioned versions of the titles, this ultimately led to his defending the IWGP Jr. Tag Team Championships alongside Kanemoto against the dynamic NOAH tandems of Tsuyoshi Kikuchi and Yoshinobu Kanemaru and, later, Marufuji and Kotaro Suzuki. At a time when all major companies were working together out of necessity, the New Japan January 4th 2004 show saw the GHC Jr. Heavyweight Champion Takashi Sugiura defend his title at the Tokyo Dome against Liger. Liger endured heavy punishment and out powered Sugiura, winning with a brain buster from the top rope to begin his one reign as GHC Jr. Champion.

Defending the GHC title successfully five times in his six-month reign against diverse members of the NOAH roster, from veteran Mitsuo Momota to youngster Kotaro Suzuki across both NOAH and New Japan events. Liger showcased the championship, before losing it in the most meaningful way. On 10th July 2004 at the first NOAH run Tokyo Dome event, Liger lost to Yoshinobu Kanemaru in front of 58,000 people, further cementing Kanemaru as the ace of NOAH's junior division.

REIGNS

1. 04/01/2004 (DEFEATED: Takashi Sugiura) - 10/07/2004 (LOST TO: Yoshinobu Kanemaru)

- Combined days as champion: 188
- Combined defences: 5

8. KENTA

The tournament to crown the first GHC Jr. Heavyweight Champion was held mere weeks after the 20 year old Kenta Kobayashi had returned to action following injury. He was a first round exit and his failure served as impetus to change his name to KENTA and recommit himself to his goals.

In April 2002 another tournament was held to crown the GHC Jr. Heavyweight Champion following Marufuji´s vacating of the title and this time KENTA fared much better, reaching the finals before losing to Yoshinobu Kanemaru. In early 2003, KENTA and Marufuji started to tag together on a regular basis and participated in the tournament to crown the first ever GHC Jr. Tag Team Champions, defeating Jushin Thunder Liger and Takehiro Murahama in the finals, the two princes stood together as the dynamic peak of the junior division. During their near two-year reign, KENTA was rewarded with a seven match trial series allowing him to challenge giants like Misawa, Kobashi and Takeyama, though he was defeated at their hands his guts and never-say-die attitude won him even greater devotion.

On 18th July 2005 KENTA walked into the Tokyo Dome as the hottest wrestling talent in the world and had a perfectly paced, ever escalating war with Kanemaru, culminating in the Busaiku knee strike and KENTA being crowned GHC Jr. Heavyweight Champion. This reign saw KENTA become a truly global star battling in the States for Ring of Honor, defending the title seven times before eventually falling to Sugiura.

Between 2006 and 2009 KENTA engaged in a classic series of matches against Brian Danielson, which were bookended by brutal title matches, starting with KENTA failing to win the ROH World Title but ending in Hiroshima with victory over Danielson to win his second GHC Jr. Heavyweight Championship. KENTA held the belt for over a year, interrupted only by a two-week spell when he was shocked by Katsuhiko Nakajima at a Kensuke Office show in February, losing the belt only to win it back 18 days later in a NOAH ring. Looking unbeatable, it was a knee injury which forced KENTA to vacate the title in October 2009, his story in the new decade following his return would mostly, finally, centre around the Heavyweight Championship.

REIGNS

1. 18/07/2005 (DEFEATED: Yoshinobu Kanemaru) - 04/06/2006 (LOST TO: Takashi Sugiura)
2. 13/10/2008 (DEFEATED: Brian Danielson) - 11/02/2009 (LOST TO: Katsuhiko Nakajima)
3. 01/03/2009 (DEFEATED: Katsuhiko Nakajima)- 30/10/2009 (Vacated due to knee injury)

- Combined days as champion: 685
- Combined defences: 12

CLASSIC MATCH N°1

Date: 18th July 2005
Location: Tokyo Dome, Tokyo
Attendance: 62,000

KENTA vs YOSHINOBU KANEMARU

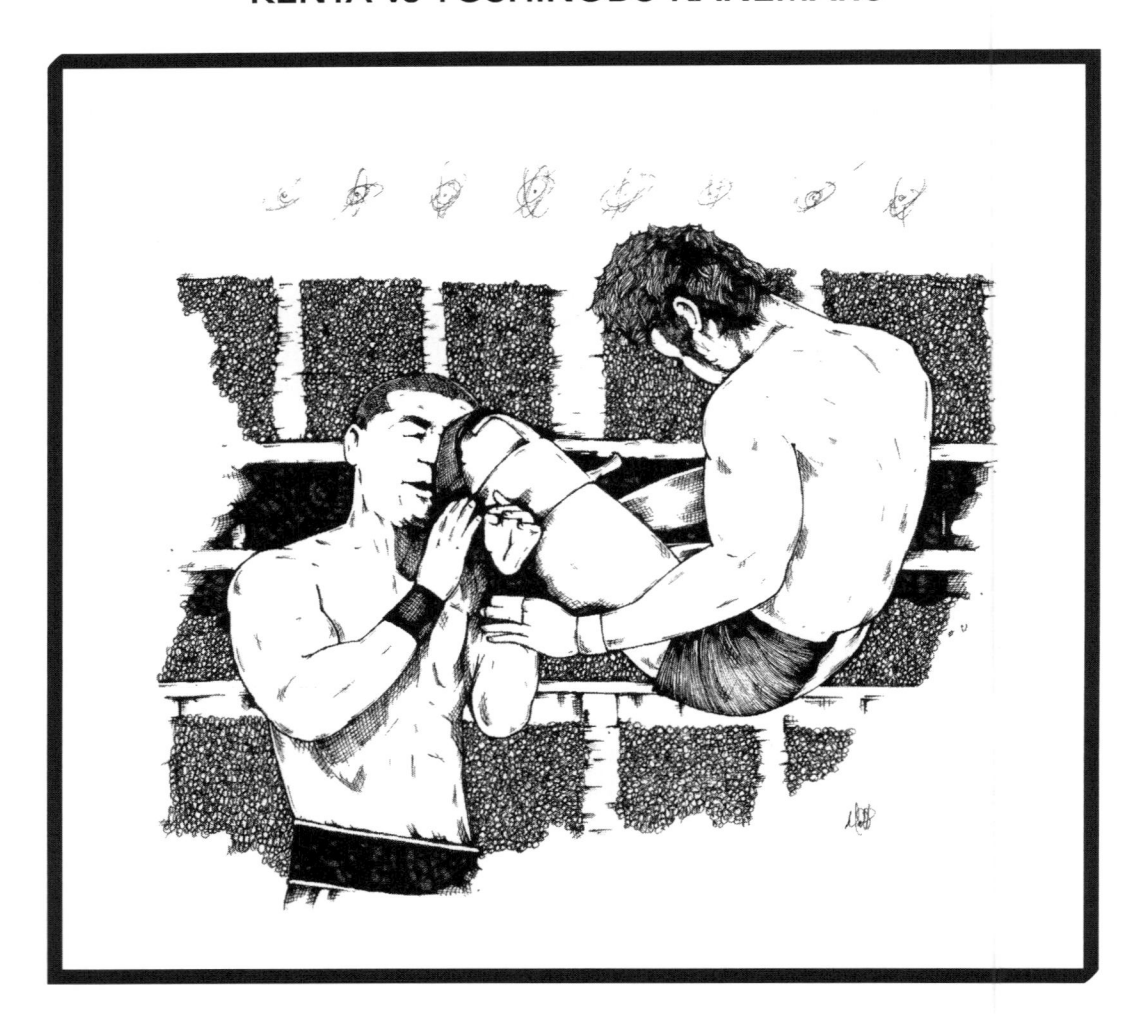

To crown a king. KENTA hits the Busaiku knee after twenty perfectly paced minutes to win the GHC Jr. Heavyweight Championship for the first time, to the delight of the sold out Tokyo Dome.

9. Mushiking Terry

Mushiking: The King of Beetles was a hybrid collectable card/arcade game first published by SEGA in 2003, with both a Mushiking manga and anime released to support the title in 2005. The titular Mushiking was, as the game's title suggests, a Japanese Rhinoceros beetle, who fought evil invading insects.

Through dynamic presentation of pure pro-wrestling NOAH found itself in 2005 the biggest wrestling company in Japan and realised the need to entice a new generation of fans to ensure continued success. A pair of characters were created in conjunction with the franchise, Mushiking Joker (portrayed by Ricky Marvin) and Mushiking Terry (portrayed by Kotaro Suzuki). Debuting both gimmicks in the Tokyo Dome on 18th July 2005, just as New Japan had debuted the similarly cartoon inspired Jushin Thunder Liger 16 years previously, NOAH could only have dreamed of a similar level of success. The hero, Terry, defeated Joker in a fun match, but was ultimately overshadowed by every subsequent match on that historic night.

By the end of August, Kotaro Suzuki was making appearances under his own name and would appear intermittently as the beetle hero over the course of the three year licensing agreement. Still fresh from his debut, Terry challenged KENTA for his GHC Jr. Heavyweight Championship in October 2005, but was soundly beaten by KENTA at his vicious best. Mushiking Terry would have to wait until April 2007 and a shock victory over Tatsuhito Takaiwa to claim his GHC Junior Championship; however, due to Kataro Suzuki's success as one half of the junior tag team championships, his beetle alter ego did not defend his title, losing it immediately to Kanemaru when he finally did. In July 2008, Mushiking's contract expired and he returned to the forest, never to be seen in NOAH again.

REIGNS
1. 28/04/2007 (DEFEATED: Tatsuhito Takaiwa) - 27/10/2007 (LOST TO: Yoshinobu Kanemaru)
• Combined days as champion: 182
• Combined defences: 0

10. Brian Danielson

Famously receiving his first pro-wrestling tutelage from Rudy Gonzalez and Shawn Michaels in San Antonio, Texas, Danielson's first exposure to Japan came immediately following his graduation from training school. Touring FMW in December 1999, he made his PPV debut from the Korakuen Hall during the visit before returning to the USA and a developmental contract with WWF. During this first spell with the company, Danielson received additional training from the great technician William Regal, forging the bright young prospect into a refined wrestler in the mould of Regal himself.

Following his release in mid-2001, Danielson won the well publicised APW King of the Indies Tournament, shortly after main-eventing the first ever Ring of Honor event before making his New Japan debut in October 2002. During lengthy tours with NJPW over the next two years Danielson captured the IWGP Jr. Tag Team Championships alongside Christopher Daniels (as Curry Man) and unsuccessfully challenged for the IWGP Jr. Heavyweight and U-30 Championships while an integral figure on the NJPW dojo shows in California.

Claiming the ROH World Title in September 2005 and embarking on a record breaking reign, Danielson committed himself full time to ROH and so, through an agreement between ROH and NOAH, came to debut for NOAH in November 2006. As ROH Champion, Danielson defended the title a record 38 times and among his most famous defences were Naomichi Marufuji and KENTA, rivalries he gleefully re-sparked in NOAH appearances between 2006 and 2009. Finally, on an ROH show held in Tokyo on 14th September 2008, Danielson battled Yoshinobu Kanemaru, and captured the GHC Jr. Heavyweight Championship, successfully defending the belt six days later back in the USA, against Katsuhiko Nakajima. However, the following month, old rival KENTA recaptured the title in front of a rapturous Hiroshima crowd, left in awe by the 30 minute classic presented to them by the two men.

After one more tour with NOAH, Danielson became Daniel Bryan on his return to the WWE, going on to become one of the most successful and universally acclaimed superstars in that company's history.

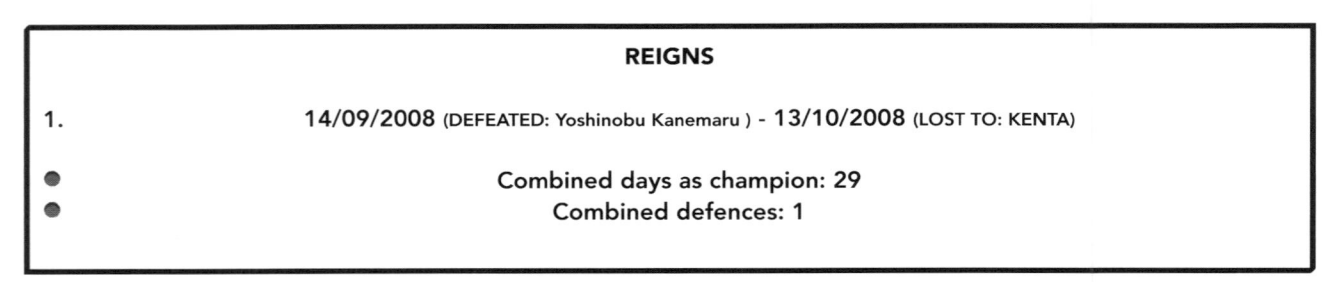

REIGNS
1.   14/09/2008 (DEFEATED: Yoshinobu Kanemaru) - 13/10/2008 (LOST TO: KENTA)
• Combined days as champion: 29
• Combined defences: 1

11. Katsuhiko Nakajima

Protege of Kensuke Sasaki, having debuted in New Japan at the age of 15 and followed his mentor to All Japan Pro-Wrestling where he became the youngest man to win their World Junior Heavyweight Championship. 2005 saw Nakajima spend time with ZERO-1, Dragon Gate, All and New Japan alongside sporadic appearances for NOAH, outshining and out-striking men with twice his age and experience.

In 2008 the Kensuke Office began to run more regular independent shows with their representatives appearing both in NOAH and All Japan, Sasaki and Nakajima appearing in NOAH's Global Tag League as a prelude to joining the company full time later in the year. On the 14th of June, Sasaki and Nakajima faced the pairing of Kenta Kobashi and KENTA, with Nakajima presented as KENTA's equal, the match went to a 30 minute time limit draw and a rivalry was set in motion. Having gained a pair of tag-team victories over KENTA, Nakajima went a step further in a brutal strike focused encounter on the 11th of February 2009 Kensuke Office show, defeating him for the GHC Jr. Heavyweight Championship. Just 18 days later KENTA gained revenge with the Go to Sleep and recaptured his title in what was a dominant year for him.

Subsequently, Nakajima would battle extensively with Kotaro Suzuki, either in tag-team contests or individually, challenging for Suzuki's Jr. Heavyweight Championship. September 2011 saw a string of tag matches culminate in a title challenge for Nakajima which he won to once more become Junior Heavyweight Champion. However, once more, his reign was short, just nine days, as he vacated the belt requiring emergency surgery for appendicitis. In his absence, Ricky Marvin won the belt, but refused to accept it unless he defeated Nakajima, who he considered the true champion. Unfortunately for the noble Marvin, Nakajima returned to NOAH on the 27th of November and gained emphatic victory, winning the title for the third time and starting a significant reign, holding the gold until the following May.

Nakajima continued to grow, in the coming years going on to tell his story in the GHC heavyweight division.

REIGNS
1. 11/02/2009 (DEFEATED: KENTA) - 01/03/2009 (LOST TO: KENTA)
2. 23/09/2011 (DEFEATED: Kotaro Suzuki) - 02/10/2011 (Vacated due to illness)
3. 27/11/2011 (DEFEATED: Ricky Marvin) - 09/05/2016 (LOST TO: Yoshinobu Kanemaru)

- Combined days as champion: 191
- Combined defences: 4

12. Kotaro Suzuki

Kotaro Suzuki graduated from the NOAH dojo, having primarily received training from Mitsuharu Misawa on Christmas Eve 2001 under his birth name Yasuhiro Suzuki. From February 2002, he became Kotaro and made progress through his early defeats, a dynamic hard-hitting high-flyer Suzuki showed early potential and, by the end of his first year, was teaming with legends like Misawa and Akiyama and his contemporaries KENTA and Marufuji.

With Marufuji he appeared in New Japan to challenge Liger and Kanemoto for the IWGP Jr. Tag Team Titles acquitting himself admirably as the two represented NOAH's dynamic, young junior division. 2004 saw Suzuki once more in the ring with Liger, unsuccessfully challenging for the GHC Jr. Heavyweight Championship for the first time, it was also the year that saw him form a highly successful team with Ricky Marvin. His first taste of singles championship success came under someone else's name, while portraying Mushiking Terry, as he had for two years, he overcame Tatsuhito Takaiwa under the mask, while one half of the tag champions as himself.

It would be approaching his 10th anniversary that Suzuki finally claimed the Jr. Heavyweight Championship for himself; having left the villainous Disobey faction and paying tribute to his recently deceased mentor Misawa though his adoption of trademark Misawa moves, Suzuki was the ultimate Junior Heavyweight hero when he defeated his former stable mate Yoshinobu Kanemaru to become champion, starting a lengthy reign in December 2010. Among those members of Burning who left NOAH in 2013, it was after a number of years with AJPW as a freelancer in which Suzuki further enhanced his reputation, that he returned to NOAH in 2018. Winning the Global Junior League to earn the right to challenge then champion Daisuke Harada, Suzuki captured the Jr. Heavyweight Championship for the second time in October 2018. Now a respected veteran, showing himself more than a match for the ever more spectacular new generation, his third reign in 2020 further cementing his status as a legend.

REIGNS

1. 05/12/2010 (DEFEATED: Yoshinobu Kanemaru) - 23/09/2011 (LOST TO: Katsuhiko Nakajima)
2. 30/10/2018 (DEFEATED: Daisuke Harada) - 16/12/2018 (LOST TO: Daisuke Harada)
3. 19/04/2020 (DEFEATED: Yoshinari Ogawa) - 08/11/2020 (LOST TO: Daisuke Harada)

- Combined days as champion: 521
- Combined defences: 14

13. Ricky Marvin

A second generation wrestler trained initially by his father, Ricardo Fuentes debuted in 1995 under the name White Demon aged just 15. An innovative high-flyer, Fuentes began working for CMLL in 1998 and adopted the Ricky Marvin name. 2000 saw Marvin's first appearances in Japan with both CMLL Japan and a loss to CIMA in the first round of the Super J Cup, hosted by Michinoku Pro, followed by a number of tours with Toryumon.

Marvin's first appearance for NOAH came in June 2003, where he proved to be well liked and he began appearing full time in 2004, forming regular tag teams with Kotaro Suzuki and Low Ki, as well as wrestling under a mask as the villainous Mushiking Joker. On 21st January 2007 the pairing of Marvin and Suzuki won the Jr. Heavyweight Tag Team Championship, the first of his three reigns with the tag belts, his second coming in 2010 alongside Taiji Ishimori and his third in 2012 with Super Crazy, but his opportunities to win the GHC Jr. Heavyweight Championship were limited.

Marvin battled KENTA to unsuccessfully challenge for his title in June 2009 and waited until May 2011 for his next title opportunity, when he was beaten by former partner Suzuki. Later in that same year, following Nakajima's vacating the title due to appendicitis, Marvin defeated Nakajima's fellow Kensuke Office member, Satoshi Kajiwara, to claim the vacant Jr. Heavyweight Title; however, Marvin in turn immediately vacated the championship, branding his victory worthless unless it were over Nakajima. Following a preview tag contest the previous night on a Kensuke Office show in which Nakajima looked as sharp as ever, he returned to NOAH on the 27th of November and regained his title by soundly defeating Marvin.

Despite never again winning the title, Ricky Marvin remained a hugely respected figure, staying full time with NOAH until AAA enticed him back to Mexico on a more regular basis from 2014 onward.

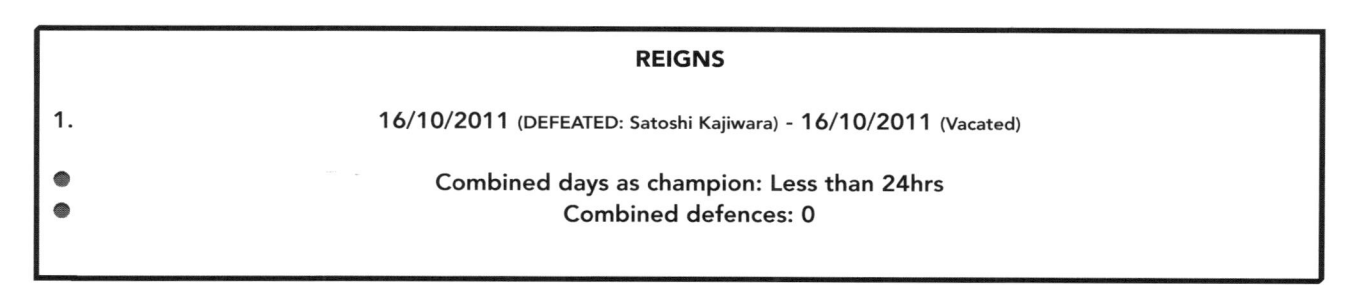

REIGNS
1.   16/10/2011 (DEFEATED: Satoshi Kajiwara) - 16/10/2011 (Vacated)
•   Combined days as champion: Less than 24hrs
•   Combined defences: 0

14. Shuji Kondo

Trained by Último Dragón, Shuji Kondo debuted for Toryumon in May 2001, a lightening quick powerhouse, the combination of his strength and speed instantly helping him stand out from his peers. A star of early Dragon Gate, his career was potentially derailed early when he and his stablemates were fired by the company for allegedly upsetting sponsors at a corporate end of year party in 2004.

Fortunately, he and long term friend YASSHI, joined forces with veteran TARU in All Japan and won the All Asia Tag Team Titles within a few months of their debut, going on to become founding members of Voodoo Murders later in the year. Remaining loyal to All Japan in the coming years Kondo's first exposure to NOAH was in trying to retake the AJPW World Jr. Heavyweight Title back from the invading Naomichi Marufuji. The near 40 min match in November 2008 saw the two innovators tear the house down in the semi-main event slot and opened the door for Kondo to work with NOAH at a later date.

His first official match in a NOAH ring took place on 15th January 2012 as he and Hiroshi Yamato defeated the team of Marufuji and Ricky Marvin, they would go on the following month to unsuccessfully challenge for the GHC Jr. Tag-Team Championships and throughout 2012 sporadically invade as AJPW representatives. In September, Kondo had his first singles match, challenging Kanemaru for the Junior Heavyweight Championship, overpowering the veteran and becoming champion in emphatic fashion. Appearing once a month in NOAH to defend his title, history was made on the 2nd of January 2013 as Kondo defeated his team mate, Hiroshi Yamato, for the AJPW World Jr. Heavyweight Title, becoming the first man to hold the NOAH and AJPW versions of the belt simultaneously.

His GHC reign lasted until 27th January 2013 when he was defeated by fellow Toryumon alumni Taiji Ishimori, Kondo going on to wrestle primarily for AJPW and Wrestle-1, appearing in NOAH only once more, in September 2018, to celebrate Marufuji's 20th anniversary as a wrestler.

REIGNS
1. 29/09/2012 (DEFEATED: Yoshinobu Kanemaru) - 27/01/2013 (LOST TO: Taiji Ishimori)
Combined days as champion: 120
Combined defences: 3

15. Taiji Ishimori

After a whirlwind four years following his 2002 debut, which saw Ishimori spend time with his home promotion Toryumon, New and All Japan and a host of independents, the spectacular, muscle bound high flyer, settled in NOAH. Debuting in the most conspicuous way possible, Ishimori challenged KENTA for the GHC Jr. Heavyweight Championship on the 23rd of April 2006 and, though unsuccessful, made an indelible impression on the champion who henceforth accepted him as a regular tag-team partner. KENTA and Ishimori won the GHC Jr. Tag-Team Championship in March 2008 and also won that year´s Junior Heavyweight Tag League; the following year Ishimori would also win the tag title with Ricky Marvin, but would consistently come up short when contending for singles honours. The impression given being that the spectacular aerialist was a benefit to a cerebral partner, but lacked the maturity to claim the Jr. Heavyweight Championship and stand alone.

In 2010 Ishimori participated in New Japan´s Best of the Super Juniors Tournament, reaching the semi final before eventual defeat at the hands of Prince Devitt. Finding success in groups ANMU and then BRAVE, Ishimori´s abilities were still not translating to singles victory, as of January 2013 he had challenged for the GHC Jr. Heavyweight Championship six times unsuccessfully, but he learnt from each stumbling block and when he finally claimed the title from Shuji Kondo, he was more than ready for it. Defending the title ten times across an epic 405 day reign (to date, still the longest in the championship´s history) against a diverse array of opponents, from Zack Sabre Jr. to Fenix, Ishimori was finally deposed by Daisuke Harada in the culmination of a thrilling rivalry.

2015 was occupied with the war against Suzuki-gun, ending triumphantly by defeating Taichi to begin his second reign. His third spell with the championship revolved around Ishimori´s rivalry with RATEL´S, defeating HAYATA in June 2017, but losing to his long-term rival Harada in December. Shortly after this defeat, having achieved all he could professionally in NOAH, Ishimori opted to continue his career by returning to New Japan.

REIGNS		
1.	27/01/2013 (DEFEATED: Shuji Kondo) - 08/03/2014 (LOST TO: Daisuke Harada)	
2.	23/12/2015 (DEFEATED: Taichi) - 24/02/2016 (LOST TO: Yoshinobu Kanemaru)	
3.	25/06/2017 (DEFEATED: HAYATA)- 01/10/2017 (LOST TO: Daisuke Harada)	
•	Combined days as champion: 566	
•	Combined defences: 12	

16. Daisuke Harada

Trained for pro-wrestling by the Osaka Pro-Wrestling dojo, Harada debuted in a losing effort against Atsushi Kotoge a man who he would alternately partner and feud with for many years to come. Harada found great success, between 2006 and 2013 when he finally left the company, he had won every championship available in Osaka Pro-Wrestling.

In February 2010 Harada debuted for NOAH in Osaka World Hall, a loss to Eddie Edwards opened the door for opportunities in the future. Later in the year Kotoge and Harada returned to participate in the Jr. Heavyweight Tag League and would appear sporadically as a team for NOAH until committing full time to the company, in Harada´s case in May 2013. Taiji Ishimori was the reigning GHC Jr. Heavyweight Champion and Harada earned the right to challenge for the belt after winning a three-way involving Ishimori and Zack Sabre Jr. in October 2013, the title match would happen in his home town of Osaka. But there was no glorious homecoming, Ishimori retained and Harada began losing every match trying to think of a way back to the title. His path was to join KENTA´s faction No Mercy, in opposition to Ishimori´s group BRAVE, leading him to another title opportunity and a classic match in March 2014 which he won, becoming GHC Heavyweight Champion for the first time.

His first challenger, in Osaka, was Kotoge, but he prevailed, holding the belt until the end of the year when his former partner challenged once more and this time succeeded in dethroning him. On Kotoge´s losing the belt the two became allies and enjoyed a dominant GHC Jr. Tag Title reign, ending as Kotoge transitioned to heavyweight. Remaining a junior, Harada founded RATEL´S, winning a number one contenders tournament in August 2017 to once more earn the right to challenge Taiji Ishimori for the Jr. Heavyweight Championship. On the 1st of October 2017, Harada became champion for the second time, keeping the belt for over a year; the title was traded back and forth between Harada and returning Kotaro Suzuki at the end of 2018, with Harada finally being defeated by legend Minoru Tanaka to end his third reign in early 2019.

Following the dissolution of RATEL'S, 2020 once more found Harada teaming with Kotoge and earning his fourth GHC Junior Heavyweight Championship. A powerful technician focused on being the best athlete and holding every championship with deserved pride, Daisuke Harada is to be considered among the best junior heavyweights of all time.

REIGNS

1. 08/03/2014 (DEFEATED: Taiji Ishimori) - 06/12/2014 (LOST TO: Atsushi Kotoge)
2. 01/10/2017 (DEFEATED: Taiji Ishimori) - 30/10/2018 (LOST TO: Kotaro Suzuki)
3. 16/12/2018 (DEFEATED: Kotaro Suzuki) - 10/03/2019 (LOST TO: Minoru Tanaka)
4. 08/11/2020 (DEFEATED: Kotaro Suzuki) - (CURRENT)

- Combined days as champion: 766+
- Combined defences: 14+

CLASSIC MATCH N°2

Date: 8th March 2014
Location: Ariake Colosseum, Tokyo
Attendance: 6,000

DAISUKE HARADA vs TAIJI ISHIMORI

The spectacular Ishimori and the grappler Harada pushed each other to the limits whenever they clashed, both helping the other grow in the process. Here, Ishimori seeks a submission before losing his title to a perfect bridging German Suplex.

17. Atsushi Kotoge

Atsushi Kotoge debuted on the 29th of April 2005 with Osaka Pro-Wresling, having graduated from their dojo. A technical high-flyer, Kotoge had a very slight build and in over a year of competing only defeated two men in singles competition, the comedic Takoyakida and the young debutant Daisuke Harada. The latter of whom swiftly became Kotoge´s tag partner and during their time in Osaka the pairing won three tag team championships.

Following a number of tag team appearances for NOAH and without the single´s obligations which bound Harada to Osaka Pro-Wrestling, Kotoge signed full time for the company in 2012 and debuted to great fanfare against standard bearing heavyweight, Go Shiozaki. Kotoge lost, but showed great spirit at a size and experience disadvantage, and following this match went undefeated for a month before challenging for the GHC Jr. Heavyweight Championship. Again, despite being defeated, Kotoge rebounded and joined Marufuji´s BRAVE faction, winning the 2012 Junior Tag League alongside stablemate Ishimori.

When Harada joined Kotoge in NOAH Kotoge was at pains to put himself at odds with his former friend, defeating him in his debut and remaining on opposite sides as Harada joined KENTA´s group No Mercy, feuding with BRAVE. Kotoge unsuccessfully challenged HARADA for the GHC Jr. Heavyweight Championship in April 2014, before finally standing tall over him in December, beating him to win the title for himself. Managing one defence, again over Harada, Kotoge´s reign ended with the invasion of Suzuki-gun and the arrival of Taichi.

Reunited with Harada over the following year, the two enjoyed great success, Kotoge winning the Junior Heavyweight Championship one more time in October 2016 and the Junior tag titles in December, becoming a double champion in the process. However, just two days after the tag victory, he vacated both of his Junior Championships to continue his story in the heavyweight division.

REIGNS
1. 06/12/2014 (DEFEATED: Daisuke Harada) - 15/03/2015 (LOST TO: Taichi)
2. 23/09/2016 (DEFEATED: Yoshinobu Kanemaru) - 26/12/2016 (Vacated to move to the heavyweight division)
• Combined days as champion: 193
• Combined defences: 4

18. Taichi

Taichiro Maki graduated from the All Japan dojo and made his debut under the name Taichi Ishikari on the 2nd of December 2002. During the first year of his career, he appeared for AJPW and ZERO-1 extensively, reaching the final of the latter´s Lion King Cup in 2003 before making his first international appearance, representing Japan in NWA-TNA´s World X Cup the following year.

Ishikari first challenged for gold unsuccessfully when fighting Taka Michinoku for the AJPW World Jr. Heavyweight Title in September 2005, after which he wrestled independently before signing with New Japan one year later. During this period with the company, Ishikari was dropped from his name and Taichi found most regular success as part of a tag team with Milano Collection AT, Unione, challenging for the Jr. Heavyweight Titles on a number of occasions.

Following Milano´s retirement in 2010, Taichi spent a number of months in Mexico with CMLL, teaming with fellow NJPW wrestlers on excursion and feuding with the popular Mexican star Máximo. On his return to NJPW, Taichi joined Kojima-gun, a faction led by then IWGP Heavyweight champion Satoshi Kojima, who was betrayed by his group on May 3rd 2011. With everyone rejecting Kojima to follow the vicious Minoru Suzuki, Kojima-gun became Suzuki-gun in an instant and a dominant force was born.

As part of the faction, Taichi and Taka Michinoku won the IWGP Jr. Heavyweight Tag Titles and participated in a full scale invasion of rival company NOAH in January 2015. With Suzuki-gun members instantly put into contention for GHC Titles, Taichi first defeated Zack Sabre Jr. to become n°1 contender and then toppled Atsushi Kotoge to become GHC Jr. Heavyweight Champion. He retained the belt through nefarious tactics until the end of the year, when the heroic Ishimori brought his dark reign to an end. After one more year with NOAH, Suzuki-gun would return to New Japan and Taichi soon after joined the heavyweight ranks.

REIGNS
1. 15/03/2015 (DEFEATED: Atsushi Kotoge) - 23/12/2015 (LOST TO: Taiji Ishimori)
Combined days as champion: 283
Combined defences: 4

19. Hajime Ohara

Under the instruction of Último Dragón, Ohara made his pro-wrestling debut for Toryumon Mexico in 2004, initially feuding and teaming with a young Kazuchika Okada, who defeated him in the first round of the 2004 Young Dragons Cup and the finals of the same competition in 2005. Working with a range of Mexican companies, from minor independents to international monolith CMLL, Ohara also participated in MMA competition, which fed into his pro-wrestling work as an exemplary junior heavyweight technician.

Ohara first appeared in Japan in Osaka Pro-Wrestling, alongside his trainer Último Dragón in 2007, defending his NWA World Welterweight Title, won from Fantasma Jr. the previous year. More prolonged exposure to Japanese audiences came via appearances in HUSTLE, ZERO-1 and Dradition before Ohara made his NOAH debut in May 2013.

Initially Ohara was a part of No Mercy, working under a mask as Maybach Suwa Jr., but within a few months had reverted to his real name, having lost his mask. At the end of the year, Ohara defeated Ishimori in the finals of the Matsumoto Day Clinic Cup and in doing so earned the right to challenge him for the GHC Jr. Heavyweight Championship on 19th of January 2014, but Ohara lost and Ishimori retained his title. Over the next two years Ohara formed a successful partnership with Kenoh, winning the GHC Jr. Tag Titles twice, until the junior division was shaken up by Kotoge's vacating of his championship in January 2017.

There was no tournament to crown a new champion, instead Ohara fought Taiji Ishimori with the winner to be awarded the belt, Ohara subsequently overcame Ishimori in a hard-hitting encounter on 13th of January. Ohara held the belt until May, defending it twice in battles against Daisuke Harada and Hitoshi Kumano, before being upset by the dynamic HAYATA. In the years following Ohara would focus more on the junior tag team division, forming the successful Back Breakers team with former rival Hitoshi Kumano.

REIGNS
1.   07/01/2017 (DEFEATED: Taiji Ishimori) - 27/05/2017 (LOST TO: HAYATA)
Combined days as champion: 140
Combined defences: 2

20. HAYATA

HAYATA debuted in 2006 having received training from independent star Hanzo Nakajima, making appearances in his early years for DDT Pro, AJPW and ZERO-1, before settling on Osaka Pro-Wrestling as his home promotion. After three years with the company, HAYATA and a number of other OPW wrestlers saw room in the Osaka market for a new independent promotion, breaking away from Osaka Pro they formed Doutonbori Pro-Wrestling and it was on their first show that HAYATA first teamed with equally enigmatic soul Yo-Hey.

Gaining renown as a spectacular tag team, the pair wrestled all over the Japanese independent scene together for the next four years, HAYATA broadening his cv even further by participating in death matches in Pro-Wrestling FREEDOMS before making his NOAH debut in December 2016. He was swiftly joined in the new year by Yo-Hey, with whom, along with fellow Osaka Pro veterans Tadasuke and Daisuke Harada, HAYATA formed the faction RATEL´S.

It was in May of 2017 that HAYATA pinned the reigning GHC Jr. Heavyweight Champion, Ohara, in a six-man tag match, leading to a title contest the following day. On 27th of May 2017, in Osaka, HAYATA pinned Ohara to become champion for the first time, his first career singles title, though the reign was not a long one. Just one month later, in his first defence, HAYATA was toppled by Ishimori and returned to focus on tag team competition, winning the Global Jr. Heavyweight Tag League with Yo-Hey in both 2017 and 2018. After winning the Global Junior League by himself in 2019, HAYATA earned the right to challenge the legendary Minoru Tanaka in early August for the Junior Heavyweight Championship. Emerging victorious on NOAH´s 19th Anniversary Show, HAYATA was fully endorsed as the future of the division by Naomichi Marufuji as he began his second reign with the title.

REIGNS

1. 27/05/2017 (DEFEATED: Hajime Ohara) - 25/06/2017 (LOST TO: Taiji Ishimori)
2. 04/08/2019 (DEFEATED: Minoru Tanaka) - 04/01/2020 (LOST TO: Yoshinari Ogawa)

Combined days as champion: 182
Combined defences: 3

21. Minoru Tanaka

Following his enormously successful run with New Japan, Minoru's next home promotion was All Japan, where he enlisted as a member of Voodoo Murders and was placed in instant contention for the World Jr. Heavyweight Championship. After 4 years with AJPW, WRESTLE-1 became his base for the next 2, with Minoru eventually becoming a true freelancer in 2017, all the while being situated as a championship contender wherever he roamed.

As a freelancer, Minoru arrived in NOAH, in October 2017, feuding with RATEL'S and GHC Jr. Heavyweight Champion Daisuke Harada, his first title match came on the 22nd of December, with Harada bolstering his own credibility greatly with a successful defence. Forming tag teams with veteran Yoshinari Ogawa and Hi69, Minoru became a two time Junior Tag Team Champion in the space of a few months in 2018, his second reign keeping him in the orbit of Daisuke Harada as he and Hi69 feuded with RATEL'S. Entering his 25th year as a professional wrestler, Minoru once more challenged Harada, on the 10th of March 2019, this time emerging victorious to become the new Jr. Heavyweight Champion, only the second person in history (behind Marufuji) to win the GHC, IWGP and AJPW versions of the title.

Holding the championship until August 2019, Minoru Tanaka was a proud champion, doing all he could as an ambassador for NOAH whilst holding the belt, his time with it culminating perfectly in the passing of the torch to a new generation of junior stars.

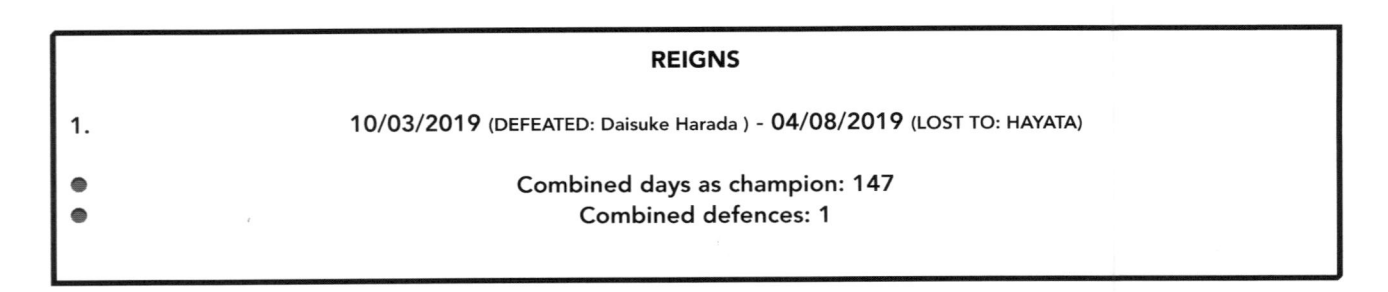

REIGNS
1. 10/03/2019 (DEFEATED: Daisuke Harada) - 04/08/2019 (LOST TO: HAYATA)
Combined days as champion: 147
Combined defences: 1

22. Yoshinari Ogawa

Yoshinari Ogawa had stepped into the shoes of Masanobu Fuchi as the standard bearer for the AJPW Jr Heavyweight division and had been champion for almost two years when he relinquished the title to join Pro Wrestling NOAH in June 2020. Teaming with Misawa, Ogawa had long been battling heavyweights in All Japan and this was a tendency which continued in NOAH, and without a Junior title to contend for, it seemed natural that Ogawa would fight for the GHC Heavyweight Championship. He participated in the tournament to crown the inaugural champion and eventually became the third man to win the title when he defeated long-term rival, Jun Akiyama, in 2002.

As part of WAVE, Ogawa frequently engaged in tag competition and won the GHC tag team titles on numerous occasions with Misawa. Rarely participating in singles bouts, he became a mentor figure who guided the younger generation of talent as they found their feet in NOAH; one such young man was Zack Sabre Jr, with whom Ogawa would win his first Junior Heavyweight tag title in December 2013, the duo defeating NJPW legends Jushin Thunder Liger and Tiger Mask. The pair would win the titles once more and Ogawa would go on to partner Minoru Tanaka, Kotaro Suzuki and HAYATA to win the belts on a further three occasions.

Despite his success as both a heavy and junior heavyweight tag team champion and his status as a former GHC Heavyweight Champion, Yoshinari Ogawa never once even challenged for the GHC Junior Heavyweight Championship. This changed on the 4th of January 2020 when, as leader of the villainous group, Stinger, Ogawa challenged and defeated the charismatic HAYATA to become champion for the first time in NOAH, almost 20 years since he had last held single's Junior Heavyweight gold. One successful defence against Daisuke Harada followed, before Ogawa lost the title to his stable mate and long-term friend Kotaro Suzuki in April 2020.

Continuing to elevate all those he works with, Yoshinari Ogawa remains at the heart of things, respected by friend and foe, as indispensable as ever before.

REIGNS
1. 04/01/2020 (DEFEATED: HAYATA) - 19/04/2020 (LOST TO: Kotaro Suzuki)
Combined days as champion: 106
Combined defences: 1

WWWA WORLD CHAMPIONSHIP

The first universally recognised women's wrestling world championship was won by strong woman Josephine Blatt in the 1890s and during her reign she helped popularise the sport of women's wrestling with tours throughout the US and Mexico. This same women's championship passed through 8 women's hands until arriving in those of Mildred Burke on the 28th of January 1937.

Mildred Burke held the title for almost twenty years and she was a paragon of strength, honour and courage. As champion, she started her own promotion, the World Women's Wrestling Association and built a loyal roster of highly talented female wrestlers, all affiliated with the governing body of the day the National Wrestling Alliance (NWA). Following the ugliest of divorces from her philandering husband, who held a position of power within the NWA, Mildred Burke found herself black-balled by the Alliance and subsequently double crossed out of her world championship. While June Byers became known as the NWA Women's Champion, Mildred Burke went back to the company she had created and became the first WWWA Champion.

Touring the world, the WWWA sought to bring women's professional wrestling out of the shadows to a wider audience. In November 1954 they toured Japan and sparked such a boom in women's wrestling to the extent that the All Japan Women's Pro-Wrestling association was set up to manage the independent promotions established in its wake. Politics led to the collapse of the association in the mid-sixties, but another attempt to promote women's wrestling in Japan on a broad scale was made in 1968 with the creation of All Japan Women's Pro-Wrestling Council (AJW).

Mildred Burke having long since retired, the WWWA held a tournament to decide its new World Champion in August 1970. The tournament was won by Marie Vagnone, who was subsequently booked to appear on an AJW event in October of that same year to be defeated by Aiko Kyo, the first Japanese holder of the championship and first WWWA champion of its lifetime as AJW's premiere title.

In total, 34 women held the championship between 1970 and March the 26th 2006 when AJW closed its doors for the last time and the title was retired. Some of those women changed the entire landscape of wrestling, innovating moves, angles and presentation of character in ways which have permeated into every level of the global wrestling industry. Any record of pro-wrestling champions would be incomplete without discussion of AJW and what follows are ten of the company's greatest champions to provide a glimpse of the historic promotion's influence.

1. Jackie Sato

Debuting for AJW at the age of 18 in April 1975 against her future partner Maki Ueda, Jackie Sato arrived on the scene as two important changes were taking place in AJW following the retirement of original chairman Toichi. The first change was a progressive move away from the traditional dynamic of Japanese hero and foreign villain with the aim of creating more homegrown stars and the second change was a venture into cross-media marketing, presenting wrestlers as pop-stars to attract a broader audience; both changes affecting Sato directly.

The first AJW wrestler to turn singer was Mach Wen Zhu, but following their pairing as a tag team and capturing the WWWA World Tag Championships in 1976, it was Jackie Sato and Maki Ueda, Beauty Pair, who changed AJW through song forever. Scoring top ten hit singles and becoming massively popular with high-schoolers, an entirely new audience flocked to and were inspired by AJW as a result of Beauty Pair´s success in their late 70s heyday.

Enjoying two tag reigns alongside Maki Ueda, Jackie Sato won the belts for the third time with Nancy Kumi in July 1977 and also continued to release pop songs under her own name, rising in popularity as Ueda pursued individual success as WWWA Champion. In November 1977, the first clash of the former tag champions and still pop icons took place as Sato challenged and defeated Ueda for the WWWA World Championship in a match which was the first true meeting of two home grown heroes in AJW and which attracted unprecedented interest. Sato then went on to hold the title for almost two years, the longest reign since the great Mildred Burke, putting Beauty Pair to rest in early 1979 by defeating Ueda in a match where both careers were on the line. Two more reigns followed for Sato, her time at the top ended in February 1981 by her student Jaguar Yokota, followed by her retirement from AJW in May of the same year having reached the mandatory retirement age of 25.

Five years later Sato changed the face of women's wrestling in Japan by establishing JWP (Japan Women's Pro-Wrestling), the first challenger to AJW´s monopoly, forcing AJW to improve in many areas due to the competition they provided, such as forcing them to eventually abolish the concept of a mandatory age of retirement. Jackie Sato stepped away from pro-wrestling a final time in March 1988, sadly passing away in August 1999, a trail blazer and an idol who laid the path for everybody that came after.

2. Jaguar Yokota

Trained by Jackie Sato, Rimi Yokota graduated from the AJW dojo at the age of 15, debuting for the company in June 1977. Although young, her ability shone through from her very earliest matches, full of innovation and intensity hitherto unseen.

On January 4th 1980 Yokota defeated Chino Sato to become the inaugural AJW Junior Champion and in the same year became the first AJW Champion and captured the WWWA Tag Team Titles alongside Ayumi Hori. Sweeping all before her, Yokota challenged her trainer Jackie Sato for the WWWA Singles Championship in February 1981, winning the match to become champion at just 19 years old.

Incredibly she would go on to hold the title for all but two months of the following five years, dominating her opponents with innovated moves such as the Jackhammer and Tiger Bomb, incredibly popular and overwhelmingly powerful, she seemed unbeatable. On May 7th 1983, however, she lost a mask vs title lucha de apuesta to the touring luchadora La Galáctica, to mean that she was without the title for all of 25 days before winning it back on the 1st of June. Eventually it was a shoulder injury which forced Yokota to vacate her championship and ushered her into early first retirement.

Continuing to contribute to AJW as a coach, Yokota trained and inspired a generation of women who would go on to rule the wrestling world, yet Yokota herself was not finished. With the mandatory requirement age lifted in 1990, she returned to AJW at the Tokyo Dome in November 1994 before going on to establish her own promotion, JD´Star in 1995 and join the burgeoning independent women's wrestling scene as a freelancer. Still fighting after more than forty years in the ring, Yokota remains the embodiment of victory through guts.

3. Yukari Omori

Debuting in 1980, Yukari Omori gained prominence very quickly as a tag team wrestler, winning her first gold in AJW alongside Mimi Hagiwara in November 1981 by capturing the WWWA Tag Titles. Defending the belts until summer 1982, Omori formed the dynamic Dynamite Girls immediately afterwards and recaptured the championships, teaming with Jumbo Hori to defeat the villainous pair of Devil Masami and Tarantula.

It was Devil Masami who won the 1985 tournament to find a new champion following the retirement of Jaguar Yokota, giving the heroic Omori a demon to slay. Chasing the title through early 1986, Omori developed a hard edge and ruthlessness to her work, her variations on the Piledriver bringing her sustained success; culminating in August 1986 when she defeated Masami to claim the WWWA World Championship, going on to hold the title for over a year.

As champion she re-popularised the use of the karate chop and she began to be known as the female Rikidōzan at the head of AJW. Omori´s reign at the top coincided with the rise of Crush Gals, Chigusa Nagayo and Lioness Asuka, and her masterful work as a foil to the incredibly popular Gals in singles competition against Nagayo or in tags alongside Jumbo Hori and Dump Matsumoto, ensured that the torch was passed on, burning bright, before her retirement from wrestling in 1988.

4. Crush Gals

Both Chigusa Nagayo and Lioness Asuka debuted for AJW in 1980, Asuka first under her own name, Tomoko Kitamura in May followed by Nagayo in August. Both found individual success quickly, though Kitamura, the slightly older, more confident of the two, was again first, winning the AJW Junior Championship in January 1981 and holding it for a full year before being obliged to vacate it. Changing her name to Lioness Asuka, she moved up to win the AJW Championship in 1982, while Nagayo claimed the Junior Championship in the same year.

The two first met as opponents in January 1983 and stole the show, the power and viciousness of Asuka clashing with the pure heart and fire of Nagayo, completing each other professionally, the Crush Gals team was formed. In chase of the tag titles, Crush Gals met the Dynamite Girls in battle throughout the end of 1983 and early 1984, wrestling a series of 60 minute draws, failing to clinch the victory but growing in popularity at every attempt. Since the pop success of Beauty Pair, AJW had tried to recapture mainstream magic with Golden Pair and Queen Angels, but neither team possessed the in-ring prowess of Crush Gals, who released their first pop single, The Bible of Fire on the 21st of August 1984. Four days later they finally captured the WWWA tag titles and the single went on to sell over 100,000 copies, catapulting both young women to pop idol status.

As a team Crush Gals were the centrepiece of AJW programming until 1986, with genre defining matches against Dump Matsumoto's Gokuaku Domei stable and the Jumping Bomb Angels before breaking up to pursue singles careers, Nagayo, the pure hero, continuing to feud with Dump Matsumoto until 1987. With momentum and public support behind her, Nagayo toppled Omori to win the WWWA Singles Title in October 1987 and Asuka poignantly began to give chase, finally earning the right to face her former partner in August 1988. Asuka won the match, yet Nagayo had injured her arm in the course of it and, rather than accept a tainted victory, Asuka refused to accept the championship, leaving it to be suspended until Nagayo could return fully fit for a rematch in January 1989. Asuka won to claim the title and embrace her position as champion, holding the belt until July with both her and Nagayo reaching retirement age later that year.

However, both record breaking women would return, profiting as partners and opponents, leading women's wrestling into the 21st Century, most notably with GAEA Japan, Lioness Asuka having her final match to date in 2013, while Nagayo is still wrestling, about to celebrate 40 years in the profession.

5. Bull Nakano

Debuting for AJW in 1983 at just 15 years of age under the name Keiko Nakano, she challenged for her first title on March 17th 1984. Losing to Yumi Ogura for the vacant AJW Junior Championship triggered a slide into aggression and misanthropy and, when she won a rematch for the title later in the year, the powerful young woman adopted the first name Bull.

Joining Dump Matsumoto's Gokuaku Domei stable and frequently teaming with Dump herself kept Bull in contention as she captured the AJW Title in 1985 and grew into a commanding force in her own right; from the innocent young trainee nicknamed Panda-Chan to a punk rock villain, forming her own stable Gokumon-To (Prison Gate Party) in 1988. Following the retirement of Lioness Asuka a one night tournament was held on the 4th of January 1990 in the Korakuen Hall to crown a new WWWA Champion, which Nakano won by defeating Mitsuko Nishiwaki in the final to start an astonishing three year title reign.

Although a villain, Nakano did not need to resort to weapons or cheating, relying instead on her own strength, which put her at odds with members of her own stable; so while she would battle the likes of Manami Toyota she also engaged Bison Kimura and Aja Kong in a series of titanic clashes, including a ground breaking steel cage match with Kong in November 1990 which utterly redefined women's wrestling. While WWWA Champion, Nakano travelled to Mexico to work for CMLL and in 1992 became double champion by beating Lola Gonzalez for the CMLL Women's Title. Seemingly unbeatable, it was her long time rival and former Prison Gate Party teammate, Aja Kong, who finally ended Nakano's remarkable reign in November 1992.

Staying with AJW for two more years, Nakano then started making appearances in the USA with the WWF, a decade after she and Dump Matsumoto had first wrestled for the American company in Madison Square Garden, winning the WWF World Women's Title in the Tokyo Dome in November 1994. After spending several successful years in North America, Nakano finally retired in 1997 due to severe knee damage, bringing an end to a career which had redefined what a Japanese women's wrester could aspire to achieve and the way in which those goals could be achieved, Bull Nakano remains a timeless icon of the sport.

6. Aja Kong

Inspired by Crush Gals and determined to be a hero, Erika Shishido debuted for AJW in 1986 at the age of 16 as a villain. As part of Dump Matsumoto's stable of violent misanthropes, Shishido teamed most regularly with Nobuko Kimura, capturing her first title alongside her as the pair won the AJW Tag Team Championship in April 1988 while stablemates Bull Nakano and Grizzly Iwamoto held the WWWA Tag Team Championships. On Matsumotos's retirement, Shishido renamed herself Aja Kong and continued to follow Bull Nakano as part of Bull's Prison Gate Party stable of violent women with larger than life universal appeal.

In March 1989, Kong defeated Manami Toyota to win the AJW Championship and in early 1990 captured the All Pacific title by defeating Noriyo Tateno, with her success building her up as a parallel power to her stable leader Nakano, leading to her splitting away alongside Kimura to form the tag team Jungle Jack in 1990. With Nakano winning the WWWA Championship, Aja Kong became one of her greatest rivals, with the two certainly having the most violent, memorable encounters, over the title and in tag team competition ever seen in AJW. Jungle Jack, Kong and Kimura, dominated the tag ranks, holding the WWWA Tag Titles from December 1990 until March 1992 until the pair split and Kong moved forward alone as leader of a stable of the same name, focusing her attention on defeating Bull Nakano.

In August 1992 Kong defeated Manami Toyota to win the Japan Grand Prix Tournament and subsequently went on to end Bull Nakano's remarkable title reign in November, becoming WWWA Singles Champion for the first time. An equally astonishing two and a half year reign of violent dominance followed, ended by her long time rival Manami Toyota in March 1995 before Kong won the title back in June, eventually losing it for the last time in August 1995 to Dynamite Kansai.

Subsequently, though mainly affiliated with AJW, Kong began to spread her wings, appearing for the WWF in the USA and independent promotions, from GAEA to Michinoku Pro around Japan until finally leaving AJW in 1997 to establish her own company, ARSION. Kong's second theme song for AJW included the line "God made the devil just for fun, but when he wanted the real thing he made Aja Kong"; still a lynchpin of Japanese women's wrestling, her role as monster heel has always been at odds with the warm, compassionate Erika Shishido who has transcended the character of Kong to become an internationally cherished legend, a facilitator and inspiration for multiple generations of wrestlers.

CLASSIC MATCH

Date: 14th November 1990
Location: Yokohama Bunka Gymnasium, Yokohama
Attendance: 6,200

BULL NAKANO vs AJA KONG

An uraken from Aja Kong in the midst of a clash of titans within a steel cage. Bull Nakano defends her WWWA World title, overcoming her toughest challenger and redefining women's wrestling in the process.

7. Manami Toyota

Debuting for AJW at the age of 16 in August 1987, Toyota achieved a great deal in short order, winning the 1988 Rookie of the Year award, her matches were packed with high flying and innovation and Toyota displayed innate gifts for both the physical and theatrical aspects of wrestling.

In November 1989, Toyota captured the AJW Championship to hold her first title and the following year won the All Pacific Championship while engaged in a long term feud with the members of Jungle Jack and Bull Nakano, participating in a string of breathtaking singles and tag matches in the early 90s.

Winning the IWA World Title from fellow innovator Kyoko Inoue in April 1992 and defending it in featured bouts on AJW programming for the next three years, Toyota rose in stature as the spectacular force for good, countering the combined five year power-based WWWA Championship reigns of Nakano and Kong. Recognised as among the best wrestlers in the world and with an unprecedented amount of international attention focused on AJW, Toyota rose to the top of the company by defeating Aja Kong, finishing a tremendously violent match with an avalanche Japanese Ocean Cyclone suplex to win the WWWA Championship in March 1995, the first of four reigns.

In defence of her title, the quality of Toyota´s matches exceeded anything that had been seen previously as she went to greater lengths to hold on to her belt in classics with anyone put in the ring with her. Losing the title for the last time to Kaoru Ito in July 2002, Toyota left AJW to perform with GAEA and a host of independent women's promotions for the next 15 years, ending her career on her 30th anniversary as a wrestler in 2017 with Oz Academy.

Unforgettable for the passion with which she fought, her guts and innovation, there are few wrestlers as imitated by both men and women as Toyota.

8. Kyoko Inoue

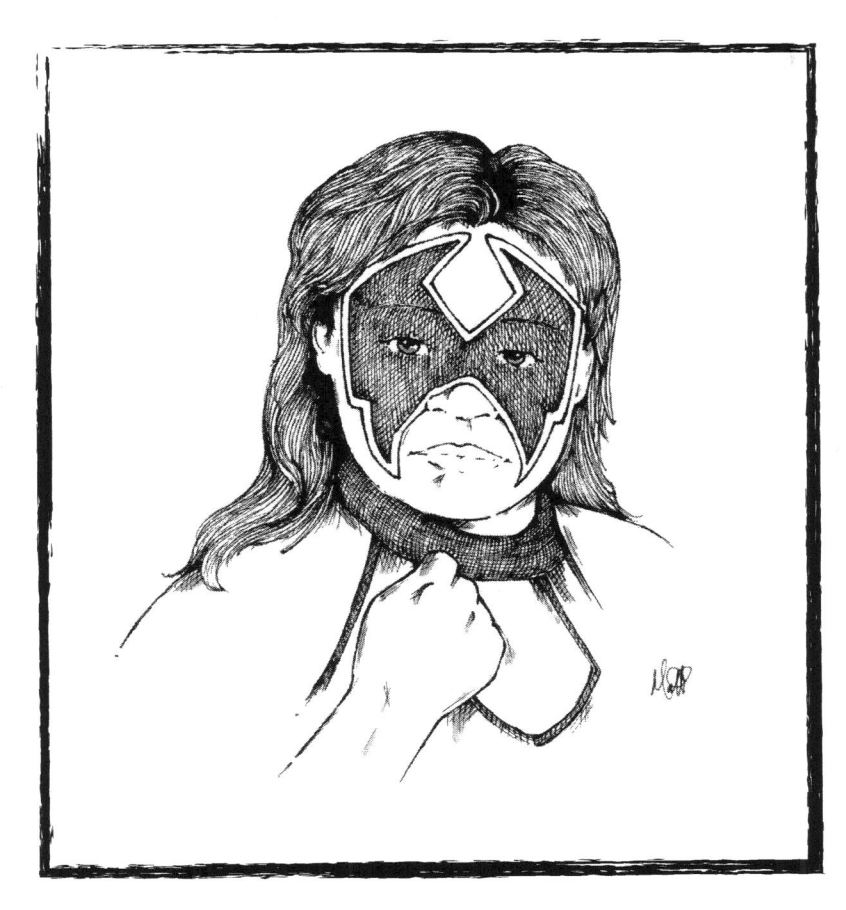

Student of Jaguar Yokota, Kyoko Inoue debuted for AJW in the Korakuen Hall against her namesake and future tag partner Takako Inoue in October 1988. Kyoko was a member of Nakano's Prison Gate Party and was directly affected by the fracturing of the alliance in 1990, forced to chose between Aja Kong and Bull Nakano, Inoue chose to stand by Nakano and partner her in epic battles against Jungle Jacks; familiarising herself with main events in the process.

Starting 1991 by winning the first ever tag team Hair vs Hair match with Nakano over Jungle Jacks, Inoue went on to win the Japan Grand Prix on August the 18th, the IWA World Title on the 31st and then challenged for the WWWA Championship for the first time in the first week of September. Despite losing, Inoue had arrived as a top star.

The following year she lost her IWA Title to Manami Toyota, which started a series of astonishing clashes between the two, Inoue being quick, resilient, powerful and innovative, in many ways Toyota's mirror, and the two made perfect opponents. In March 1994, Inoue captured the All Pacific Title, and attempted to win double gold as she challenged Alundra Blaze for the WWF Women's Title in May; however, she was unsuccessful in her attempt and Toyota defeated her for the All Pacific Title mere months later to add a further chapter to their history. In May 1995, as reigning WWWA Tag Champion, Inoue challenged Manami Toyota for the WWWA World Title; the match going to a 60-minute time-limit draw, the Korakuen Hall was exhausted after the bout, and it has long been regarded as one of the greatest wrestling matches of all time. Inoue would have to wait until December 1996 before she finally overcame her greatest rival in another classic in front of a sold out Ryogoku Kokugikan.

While champion, Inoue would unify the WWWA Championship with the IWA World Title by defeating her career long friend and rival Takako Inoue, adding further prestige to the WWWA Title, but would leave AJW shortly after. Working first for her trainer Jaguar Yokota's JD'Star promotion, before starting her own companies, NEO in 1997 and Pro-Wrestling Diana in 2011. Inoue is another tireless innovator (Kobashi was watching her tapes closely for the Burning Hammer) still wrestling having spent over 30 years in the business.

9. Ayako Hamada

Daughter of one of the most influential wrestlers in history, Gran Hamada, Ayako was born in Mexico while her father bounced between her place of birth and Japan, a top star for the UWA, EMLL and NJPW. When her father returned to Japan to work a full time schedule with Michinoku Pro-Wrestling, Ayako, then aged 14 threw herself into training, eventually joining the ARSION dojo for final guidance from Aja Kong and Mariko Yoshida.

Debuting for ARSION aged 17 in August 1998, everything seemed to come naturally to Ayako and within a year she had claimed her first title, the Twin Stars of ARSION, alongside Mika Akino. In December 2000 she toppled Aja Kong to claim ARSION's top title and become considered ace of the company while making appearances for CMLL in Mexico and a range of Japanese independent promotions from FMW to K-Dojo; her next long term base was GAEA Japan where once more she claimed the top title, acquiring the nickname Queen of the New Century in the process.

Hamada's rise to prominence came at a time when AJW was in rapid decline, the once adored promotion had lost its tv spot in March 2002 and was forced to run shows more sparingly, yet the prestige of the WWWA World Title remained, defended more frequently across the burgeoning women's independent wrestling landscape. Hamada's first WWWA Championship was won from Momoe Nakanishi in May 2003, briefly seeing her reign as a double champion by winning the WWWA Tag Titles with Nanae Takahashi from Double Inoue in January 2004.

Across her two lengthy WWWA World Championship reigns, Hamada carried the belt with her around Japan and to Mexico; one of the title's final globe-trotting champions, Hamada went on to become a major star in the USA with TNA and continues to work extensively with AAA in Mexico after a distinguished career in Japan, most notably with Pro-Wrestling WAVE.

10. Amazing Kong

Receiving primary training for pro-wrestling at the Empire Wrestling Federation's facility, the School of Hard Knocks, Kia Stevens was invited to join the AJW dojo to further her preparation in 2002. To add to her imposing aura, Stevens was renamed the Amazing Kong, paying tribute to the legendary Aja Kong who had last appeared for AJW in 1998.

Despite a loss in her debut to Yumika Hotta, Kong was otherwise a fearsome, dominant competitor in the same vein as her namesake, adopting a lot of the same mannerisms and finishing opponents with a vicious spinning back-fist. Facing Ayako Hamada in January 2004, Kong emerged victorious to become WWWA World Champion just over a year into her career, the fastest ascent to the title in company history and the first North American wrestler to win the title in 30 years. Losing the Championship back to Hamada five months later, Kong continued to work with AJW until its final show, on which she won a tag match alongside the veteran Devil Masami.

Once AJW had closed its doors for good, Kong continued to perform broadly and brilliantly around Japan, winning both singles and tag titles, having formed a dominant team with Aja Kong in 2004. She would go on to earn global superstardom in TNA and WWE and as an actress in the critically acclaimed GLOW; like so many women who have achieved incredible things, her journey involves having held the red belt, the WWWA Championship.

WORLD OF STARDOM

World Wonder Ring Stardom was founded in 2010, with three core figures behind its inception. Hiroshi "Rossy" Ogawa was the company's owner, having previously booked for AJW in its heyday and gained experience of wrestling company ownership alongside Aja Kong with the ultimately ill fated Hyper Visual Fighting Arsion. Ogawa approached Fuka Kakimoto, a retired model and wrestler, about the prospect of building a new promotion around one of her students, a gravure idol called Yuzuki Aikawa. Fuka would be recognised as the general manager of the new promotion while also undertaking responsibility for training the performers, the first wave of whom were mostly models, and getting them ready for pro-wrestling. At this stage, the help of Nanae Takahashi, veteran wrestler and the last holder of the WWWA World Championship was enlisted, to lend the new product an aura of instant credibility.

In the first year of its life Stardom held 27 shows, and attracted a number of young independent stars to sign exclusive contracts with the company. Having established an audience, Stardom introduced its top title on 27th July 2011, via a one night tournament featuring Nanae Takahashi, Mercedes Martinez, Yoko Bito and Mika Nagano, with Takahashi defeating Yoko Bito in the final to become the inaugural champion. Named the World of Stardom Championship, the strap is deliberately a particular shade of red in order to mimic and evoke memories of the WWWA World Title, with Hiroshi Ogawa on record as saying that AJW in its peak years represented the golden age of women's pro-wrestling.

Approaching a decade since Stardom´s inception, the company has experienced continued growth in popularity, having overcome difficult times and shifted focus to concentrate as much on breathtaking wrestling as on the beauty of its protagonists to the extent that the company has become a byword for the premier brand of women´s wrestling in the world. Consequently, The World of Stardom Championship can be seen as its premier title. As the company is poised to enter its second decade with live shows booked internationally and with a popular online streaming service broadcasting shows globally, Stardom and The World of Stardom might yet grow to eclipse the AJW and WWWA Championship in terms of success and influence.

1. Nanae Takahashi

Debuting on the 14th of July 1996 at the age of 15 against her future tag partner Momoe Nakanishi, Takahashi was one of the last true greats to get their start in AJW. With Nakanishi, as Nanamomo, the pair captured their first of four Tag Championships on November 23rd 1997; in total, Takahashi would win the WWWA Tag Titles five times with four different partners, before focusing on singles glory, winning the WWWA World Title twice. A Jaguar Yokota and Kyoko Inoue of her day, there is a great injustice in her victories coming at a time when AJW was without tv and that her final title win for the company came after it had closed down, defeating Kumiko Maekawa for the belt, just to immediately return it to the company president in order for it to be decommissioned.

Following AJW´s closure in April 2005, Takahashi´s indomitable entrepreneurial spirit came to the fore, whilst working for a wide range of promotions and collecting world titles, she also began her own company, Pro-Wrestling SUN, which ran as a sister promotion to ZERO-1 between 2006 and 2008. Takahashi entered 2010 as one of the most respected women in wrestling and announced in September of that year that she would be a founding member of new promotion, World Wonder Ring Stardom.

On the winning team of the first ever match in a Stardom ring, Takahashi enjoyed a successful first half of the year, building up to her 15th anniversary show in the Korakuen Hall in July 2011, which would feature a tournament to crown the first World of Stardom Champion. Takahashi defeated Mercedes Martinez and Yoko Bito on her way to victory and became the first ever champion by doing so.

No longer toiling in shadows, Takahashi had gone from final AJW champion to first World of Stardom Champion, and her reign to establish the belt´s lineage was astonishing. Holding the title for a year and a half, Takahashi continued to travel widely as champion, generating respect and intrigue in her new promotion, but this came to an end with the arrival of Alpha Female, who beat her and took her title in March 2013. Staying with the company for the following two years, Takahashi turned her focus to the issue of helping young talent establish themselves and move up the card.

Officially leaving Stardom in mid-2015, Takahashi once more created her own company, Seadlinnng, and continues to wrestle at the very top level, having provided Stardom the most solid foundation to build upon.

REIGNS
1.   24/07/2011 (DEFEATED: Yoko Bito) - 17/03/2013 (LOST TO: Alpha Female)
Combined days as champion: 602
Combined defences: 7

2. Alpha Female

Marie Gabert debuted as a wrestler under the name Jazzy Bi for the German Wrestling federation in April 2001. A towering strong-woman with a distinct look and devastating power offence, Jazzy toured Europe extensively in the following years, building a formidable reputation. Adopting the name Alpha Female in 2007 and developing an even fiercer in-ring attitude, she claimed her first title in Bilbao the following year when she defeated Lisa Schianto for the EWE Female Championship and in subsequent years added to it with the Turkish Power Wrestling's Ladies Championship and that of the UK's Pro-Wrestling EVE, before making her first trip to Japan.

Making her Japanese debut in 2012 with over a decade of experience, Alpha Female towered over her competition and went straight into contention for the World of Stardom Championship, in only her second match for the company she challenged for the title and pushed Nanae Takahashi to a 30-minute time limit draw. Having spent the winter in Europe, Alpha Female returned in March 2013 to challenge Takahashi once more, this time claiming victory and the World of Stardom Championship in the main event in front of a sold out Korakuen Hall.

Just over a month later, in her first defence, she was defeated by Io Shirai to lose the title before returning to Europe; though Alpha Female continued to find success in Stardom whenever she returned, holding both Artist and Goddess of Stardom Championships. Although her reign as champion was short, the Alpha Female was a necessary agent of evolution for the company, bringing its first chapter to a close, she forcibly turned the page to start the next, before continuing her career as a true international superstar.

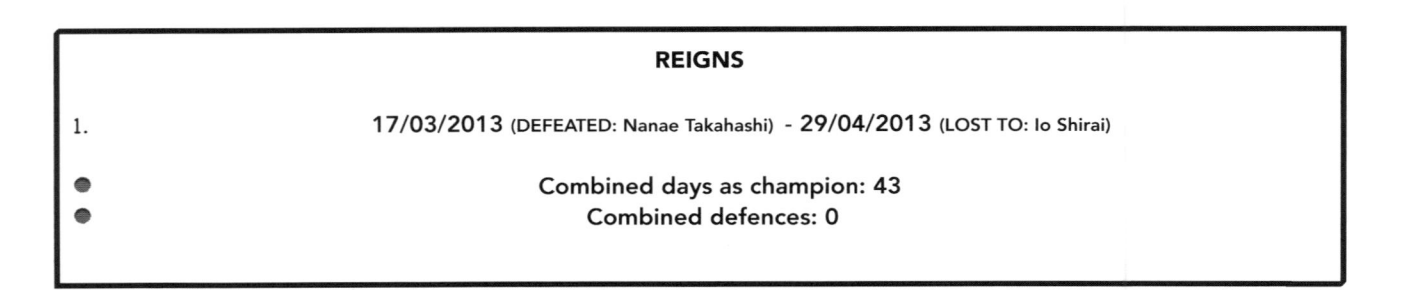

REIGNS
1. 17/03/2013 (DEFEATED: Nanae Takahashi) - 29/04/2013 (LOST TO: Io Shirai)
Combined days as champion: 43
Combined defences: 0

3. Io Shirai

Masami Odate debuted on the Japanese independent circuit at the age of 16 in early 2007. Adopting the name Io Shirai she frequently teamed with her older sister Mio, working for a wide range of promotions in their debut year. The pair's high speed, high flying helped them make names for themselves very quickly and, with the dissolution of Nanae Takahashi's Passion Red stable, the sisters adopted Kana, continuing to build their reputations together under the name Triple Tails.

In late 2010, the sisters made their debuts in Mexico for AAA, with Io continuing to take Mexican bookings into 2011, her experience in the country further helping her develop her already breathtaking abilities. On the 23rd of July 2011, Triple Tails announced that they would each go their separate ways and, 3 months later, Io made her first appearance for Stardom, tagging with then champion Nanae Takahashi to defeat Yoko Bito and Yuzuki Aikawa.

The world traveled Shirai was a major signing for the company when she became a full time talent in 2012, leading her own group called Planet and forming a dynamic team with Mayu Iwatani called Thunder Rock, all helping her grow in authority. In early 2013, Io won a n° 1 contenders tournament, earning her the right to challenge Alpha Female for the World of Stardom Championship in April. The match took place before 5,500 people in a sold out Ryogoku Kokugikan, Stardom's biggest show to date and Io emerged victorious, starting a new era for the company and an astonishing title reign which lasted almost a year and a half, consisting of ten successful defences; Io was unquestionably positioned as the ace of the company, an image which persisted long after she lost the title to Yoshiko in August 2014.

It was as ace and defender of Stardom that Io claimed her second World of Stardom Championship. Stardom had engaged in an inter-promotional feud with Meiko Satomura's Sendai Girls promotion throughout the end of 2015 with Satomura winning Stardom's top prize in July. It would be Io Shirai who stepped forward to bring the championship back home in December and begin a reign which even managed to exceed the brilliance of her first, an 18 month spell by the end of which Shirai was being lauded as the best wrestler in the world. It was her former partner Mayu Iwatani who eventually dethroned her in June 2017, yet Shirai became Artist and Wonder of Stardom Champion within a matter of months, creating the sensation that there was nothing new for her to achieve. As such, at the peak of her powers, she announced her departure for the WWE in Summer 2018.

REIGNS

1. 29/04/2013 (DEFEATED: Alpha Female) - 10/08/2014 (LOST TO: Yoshiko)
2. 23/12/2015 (DEFEATED: Meiko Satomura) - 21/06/2017 (LOST TO: Mayu Iwatani)

- Combined days as champion: 1,014
- Combined defences: 24

CLASSIC MATCH N°1

Date: 29th April 2013
Location: Ryogoku Kokugikan, Tokyo
Attendance: 5,500

ALPHA FEMALE vs IO SHIRAI

The Alpha Female tried her hardest to ground the genius of the sky in her defence of the World of Stardom Championship, yet Io Shirai would not be held down. Winning the match, Io continued to fly high, raising the standard and stature of the

4. Yoshiko

Yoshiko was among the first group of wrestlers to pass through the Stardom dojo system and had her debut match on Stardom's first show, January 23rd 2011. An aggressive, loud-mouthed villain, Yoshiko represented the brashness of youth and also its brilliance, presented as the polar opposite of the idol Yuzuki Aikawa, Yoshiko lost out to her in decision matches to crown the inaugural Wonder of and Goddess of Stardom Champions.

Despite this, Yoshiko built momentum throughout the first year of Stardom and, on the 11th of December 2011, won the Rookie of the Year Tournament. In August 2012 she unsuccessfully challenged one of her trainers, Nanae Takahashi, for the World of Stardom Championship but bounced back by teaming with another former Passion Red member Natsuki Taiyo to win her first title, the Goddesses of Stardom in November, holding the belt until March the following year.

2013 saw Yoshiko retire her first rival Yuzuki Aikawa, unsuccessfully challenge new World of Stardom Champion Io Shirai and appear for DDT-Pro, Sendai Girls and WRESTLE-1 in addition to Stardom, the young star was still on the rise and she would reach her zenith in 2014. In front of 1,000 people at the Korakuen Hall on the 10th of August 2014 Yoshiko deservedly overcame the tenacious Io Shirai to become World of Stardom Champion and begin what should have been a lengthy reign on top of the company. It certainly started well, but dominant wins over Saki Akai and Nanae Takahashi were to be followed by her third defence against former ally, Act Yasukawa, a match booked for the Korakuen on the 22nd of February 2015.

Sadly the match went horribly wrong; seemingly reacting badly to a mishap early in the match, though her exact motivations remain unclear, Yoshiko proceeded to abuse Yasukawa in the ring, beating her severely and leaving her with a horrific list of injuries including multiple broken bones and permanently impaired vision, all in front of a sickened audience and rolling tv cameras, the match being called off by officials around the ring who separated the two. Having brought the company and the World of Stardom Championship into disrepute through such gross unprofessionalism, Yoshiko was stripped of the title and suspended indefinitely, officially leaving Stardom in the summer.

REIGNS
1. 10/08/2014 (DEFEATED: Io Shirai) - 25/02/2015 (Vacated as a disciplinary measure)
Combined days as champion: 199
Combined defences: 2

5. Kairi Hojo

With a sporting history in yachting, which would later lead to her being dubbed the Pirate Princess, Hojo came to wrestling via theatre. In a case of life mimicking art, Fuka Kakimoto saw Kairi performing the role of a wrestler in a theatre production and was so impressed that she invited her to a Stardom show which led to her enrolling in the Stardom dojo. Kairi fell in love with and quickly adapted to the life of a wrestler, graduating with Stardom´s third batch of in-house trainees and debuting in January 2012.

With her aptitude and enthusiasm for wrestling shining through, Hojo won her first match after three months by defeating Mayu Iwatani, going on to do well in the Five Star Grand Prix and finishing her first year by reaching the semi-final of the 2012 Rookie of the Year Tournament. Hojo won her first championship, The Goddesses of Stardom Title, in April 2013 alongside Natsumi Showzuki, yet the reign was cut short when Showzuki incurred a severe spinal injury, leading the pair to vacate the titles and Showzuki to retire from wrestling.In 2014, with the younger members of Stardom's roster battling those born in the Shōwa period (1926-1989) Hojo found herself, at the age of 26, on the older women's team. As such, she teamed with veteran Nanae Takahashi to win the Goddesses of Stardom Titles on August the 10th, until once more being force to vacate them due to injury to her partner, Takahashi having damaged her ankle in early 2015.

Following Yoshiko´s being stripped of The World of Stardom Championship, a tournament was held to name her successor and, defeating Kyoko Kimura and Io Shirai on the same night, the 29th of March 2015, Kairi Hojo became World of Stardom Champion. A unifying figure behind the scenes and a strong hero in the ring, Kairi was the perfect champion to lead the promotion out of the turbulent times it was experiencing, her title victory made all the more poignant as she wept to end the Samurai! TV broadcast. Three successful World of Stardom defences followed, including a classic 30-minute time limit draw with Meiko Satomura which led to a rematch in July that Satomura won, ending Hojo´s title reign.

Hojo won the subsequent 5 Star Grand Prix, and the n°1 contendership, but was defeated by her great rival Io Shirai at Stardom´s 5th Anniversary show to start 2016. Hojo remained on top in Stardom, winning Artist, Goddess and Wonder of Stardom Titles before sailing further afield, signing with the WWE in mid-2017 and becoming a truly internationally adored performer.

REIGNS
1.   29/03/2015 (DEFEATED: Io Shirai) - 26/07/2015 (LOST TO: Meiko Satomura)
Combined days as champion: 119
Combined defences: 3

CLASSIC MATCH N°2

Date: 29th March 2015
Location: Korakuen Hall, Tokyo
Attendance: 965

IO SHIRAI vs KAIRI HOJO

Tears of a pirate princess on earning her treasure. After a hard fought match, overcoming Io Shirai in the tournament final, Kairi Hojo captures the World of Stardom gold and restores some of its lost lustre.

6. Meiko Satomura

Trained by Crush Gals' Chigusa Nagayo, Meiko Satormura debuted against fellow trainee and future rival/partner Sonoko Kato on April 15th 1995 for Nagayo's GAEA promotion. GAEA would remain Satomura's base in the coming years as she gained broad experience of Japanese promotions and the United States by making appearances everywhere from Michinoku Pro-Wrestling to WCW. Such experience helped her rise to the top of GAEA as AAAW Tag Team and Singles Champion, main-eventing the company's final show on 10th of April 2005 by defeating her legendary trainer.

On GAEA's closure, Satomura formed her own promotion in conjunction with Jinsei Shinzaki's Michinoku Pro-Wrestling, sharing much of the same spirit, that of exemplary wrestling combined with good humour and a positive atmosphere. After a year of training her first wave of recruits, Sendai Girls opened its doors in July 2006 with Satomura defeating Aja Kong in the main event of the first show.

Following six years of building Sendai Girls up as one of the best independent promotions in Japan, bolstered by continued travels around the country and the world, Meiko Satomura made her first appearance in Stardom; as the former ace of GAEA she challenged the final ace of AJW, Nanae Takahashi, for the World of Stardom Title. Unsuccessful in her first challenge, Satomura would appear for Stardom sporadically in the following years, always stealing the show when she did. Her appearances culminated in 2015 when she first pushed reigning World of Stardom champion Kairi Hojo to a time limit draw in June and then returned in July to win a rematch and with it, the World of Stardom Championship. In her 20th year a pro-wrestler, Satomura briefly reigned as the double World of Stardom and Sendai Girls World Champion, the undisputed queen of the sport, rightfully standing atop both companies as their inter-promotional feud continued.

Satomura's reign was ended by Stardom's most exhilarating talent, Io Shirai, in a remarkable match on the 23rd of December 2015 and she reverted her attention to her own company, subsequently only making appearances in Stardom on special occasions. Satomura continues to travel widely and is internationally acclaimed as one of the best wrestlers in the world.

REIGNS
1. 26/07/2015 (DEFEATED: Kairi Hojo) - 23/12/2015 (LOST TO: Io Shirai)
• Combined days as champion: 150
• Combined defences: 1

7. Mayu Iwatani

Part of the first class of Stardom trainees, Mayu Iwatani debuted for the company on its first show, losing to fellow debutant Arisa Hoshiki in January 2011. Forged by defeat like the very best in the business, it would take Iwatani until December of the same year to earn her first victory, progressing to the semifinals of the Rookie of the Year Tournament before being defeated by eventual winner Yoshiko.

Having bonded with the Stardom audience, Iwatani started 2012 with purpose, joining Io Shirai´s stable, Planet, and forming a regular tag team with her, known as Thunder Rock, all of which helped Iwatani develop and grow into a contender. Alongside Hiroyo Matsumoto and Miko Wakizawa, Iwatani captured the Artist of Stardom Championship in December 2013; after a three year wait for her first title, this reign opened the floodgates and Iwatani has seldom been without one or multiple championship belts in her possession ever since. In May 2015, she and Io won the Goddesses of Stardom Titles and held them for over a year, in October 2015 she won the High Speed Championship and similarly held it for over a year, her success was such that by mid-2017 Iwatani was held alongside Io Shirai and Kairi Hojo among the best wrestlers in the world, yet, unlike the other two, Iwatani had not won the World of Stardom Championship.

Finally, having defeated Kairi Hojo in May to become Wonder of Stardom Champion, she went on to beat Io Shirai in June to win the World of Stardom, holding and defending the two main singles titles simultaneously. Sustaining a hectic schedule in defence of both belts, the culmination of her six years as one of the hardest working wrestlers in her or any other company was cruelly cut short by injury. Having lost her Wonder of Stardom Championship the night before to Yoko Bito, Iwatani faced Toni Storm on the 24th of September 2017 and, just two minutes into the match, suffered a dislocated shoulder which led the referee to ring the bell and award the title to Storm, ending Iwatani´s reign after just three months.

Returning from her injury at the very end of 2017, Iwatani went on to reign as a Goddess and Artist of Stardom Champion in addition to becoming only the third ever Women of Honour World Champion. Defeating Bea Priestley in November 2019, Iwatani embarked upon her second World of Stardom championship reign, spending over a year as champion, she carried both belt and company through the difficulties of 2020 with an intense dignity indicative of the greatest champions.

REIGNS
1. 21/06/2017 (DEFEATED: Io Shirai) - 24/09/2017 (LOST TO: Toni Storm)
2. 04/11/2019 (DEFEATED: Bea Priestley) - 15/11/2020 (LOST TO: Utami Hayashishita)
• Combined days as champion: 472
• Combined defences: 7

8. Toni Storm

Initially trained for pro-wrestling by Impact Pro-Wrestling in Queensland, Australia, Toni Rossall made her debut for the company under the name Storm in October 2009, just over a week before her 14th birthday. After four years of hard work around Australia, Storm made her first appearances in Japan, making use of her first name for the first time, Toni Storm participated in two REINA international events in 2013; shows which further encouraged Storm to see the world. In order to pursue her chosen career to the fullest extent, Storm relocated to the North of England in 2014 and proceeded to work extensively around Europe, honing her talents until she was recognised among the best on the continent.

Invited to appear on Stardom's first European shows, co-hosted by the Catalan company RCW in May 2016, Toni Storm opened a lot of eyes by reaching the finals of a one-night tournament to crown the undisputed SWA Women's Champion, ultimately losing to Io Shirai. Storm made such an impression on Stardom management that within two months she was making her debut for the company in Japan, making a huge splash by defeating Io Shirai for the SWA Championship at the end of July 2016, she was presented as a highly credible threat to the best Stardom wrestlers.

Returning to Stardom throughout 2017, Storm won the Spring Cinderella Tournament by defeating Mayu Iwatani in the final and she went to a 30-minute draw with Shirai over the World of Stardom Title in May. The Summer was remarkable for Storm, seeing her win the PROGRESS Women's Championship, debuting for the WWE and winning Stardom's Five Star Tournament to earn the right to face Mayu Iwatani for the World of Stardom Championship in September. Though the manner of Storm's victory was the unfortunate injury to her opponent, few could doubt that, on paper, Storm deserved the win and the two-minute bout ended with Toni Storm declared the new champion.

Travelling the world as champion, while also WXW and PROGRESS Women's Champion, Toni Storm outclassed everybody until Summer 2018 when she was finally overturned by Kagetsu. After which, Toni Storm signed with the WWE, celebrating her arrival in the company by winning the 2018 Mae Young Classic, defeating Io Shirai in the final. The world remains Storm's for the taking.

REIGNS
1. 24/09/2017 (DEFEATED: Mayu Iwatani) - 09/06/2018 (LOST TO: Kagetsu)
• Combined days as champion: 258
• Combined defences: 3

9. Kagetsu

A student of Meiko Satomura, Kagetsu debuted for Sendai Girls under her own name of Yukari Ishino in July 2008. Enduring a challenging debut year of defeats, it would only be when partnering with her trainer that Ishino appeared on the winning side and it was December 2009 by the time she claimed her first singles victory in her home promotion.

Entering the new decade, Ishino became Kagetsu and, though Sendai Girls remained her base of operations, Kagetsu proceeded to work with the widest range of promotions and opponents as possible, helping create a truly unique wrestler capable of adapting to any style and excelling at almost everything. In March 2011, Kagetsu claimed her first championships, defeating Hiren in JWP to claim both the JWP Junior and Princess of Pro-Wrestling Titles, proceeding to defend the belts across JWP, ICE Ribbon and Sendai Girls, she would hold onto them until July before defeat to Sawako Shimono.

One among many companies for whom Kagetsu appeared in 2012 was Stardom, as she lost a one-off appearance to Saki Kashima, going on to wrestle a solitary match a year for Stardom in 2013 and 2014. Whilst still an independent wrestler, she gradually began to appear more frequently in the company, her status bolstered as she joined the Oedo Tai stable and captured her first Stardom title alongside its founder and leader Kyoko Kimura, winning the Goddesses of Stardom belts in August 2016. In 2017 Kagetsu assumed leadership of the faction on Kimura's retirement and signed a full time contract with Stardom, once more winning the Goddesses of Stardom Titles, this time alongside Hana Kimura, Kyoko's daughter.

Her position as faction leader allowed Kagetsu to demonstrate her full range as a performer, from motherly warmth and humour with her allies to vicious violence toward everyone else, whilst remaining as versatile in the ring as ever. In July 2018, Kagetsu challenged and defeated Toni Storm to begin one of the greatest World of Stardom reigns; lasting almost a year and comprised of 8 defences, Kagetsu carried the company on her back as key roster members moved on and new talent needed time to develop. Losing the belt in May 2019, Kagetsu announced her retirement from wrestling with the onset of the new year.

REIGNS
1. 09/06/2018 (DEFEATED: Toni Storm) - 04/05/2019 (LOST TO: Bea Priestley)
Combined days as champion: 329
Combined defences: 8

10. Bea Priestley

Receiving initial preparation for pro-wrestling with New Zealand Wide Pro-Wrestling whilst a resident in the country, Bea Priestley returned to the UK to develop her skills further, primarily receiving training from PROGRESS. Working extensively around the United Kingdom, 2017 saw her become most well known for her work in PROGRESS and What Culture Pro-Wrestling, for whom she won her first championship in February of that year, Priestley developed a strong reputation as a charismatic, hard hitting performer.

As such, in October 2017, she was invited to appear for Stardom, participating alongside Kelly Klein in the 2017 Goddesses of Stardom Tag League. In her third match in Japan, Priestley unsuccessfully challenged Toni Storm for the World of Stardom Championship, immediately considered a contender she was undeterred by defeat and went on to win the Tag Tournament, beating Jungle Kyona and Yoko Bito in the final.

In 2018, she returned to Stardom, reaching the final of the Cinderella Tournament in April and officially becoming a member of the Queen´s Quest stable the same month, before losing out in the final of the 2018 edition of the Goddesses of Stardom Tag League later in the year. Bea Priestley´s forward momentum and constant development in ring showed no sign of stopping with the advent of 2019; the year started with her leading a Queens Quest team to win the Stardom Trios Tournament before returning to the UK to win the World of Sport Women's Title, in turn before returning to Japan to battle Oedo Tai´s Kagetsu for the World of Stardom Championship in May. Winning a vicious contest, Priestley became the 10th woman to ever hold the title and engaged in five successful defences against the best the company had to offer before finally being toppled by the crowd-favourte Iwatani.

REIGNS

1. 04/05/2019 (DEFEATED: Kagetsu) - 04/11/2020 (LOST TO: Mayu Iwatani)
   - Combined days as champion: 184
   - Combined defences: 5

NEO HIGH SPEED CHAMPIONSHIP

Leaving All Japan Women's Pro-Wrestling in late 1997, former WWWA champion Kyoko Inoue became an independent wrestler and declared the foundation of a new promotion. Initially intended to be called New Japan Women's Pro-Wrestling, the name was changed to avoid any confusion or legal clash with NJPW to NEO Japan Ladies Pro-Wrestling, morphing after two years of business to NEO Women's Wrestling.

Though a moderately sized independent promotion, NEO rose to prominence following the collapse of AJW and GAEA Japan, becoming seen as the pre-eminent women's wrestling promotion in Japan. In May 2009 a match was held between two lightning fast competitors, Natsuki Taiyo and Ray to add a new championship to the NEO pantheon of titles, the High Speed Championship. With business down, the new title was a means of showcasing dynamic, fast paced high flying and this match to become inaugural champion epitomised the thrilling style that would become the championship's hallmark, Natsuki Taiyo claiming victory and the gold.

Unfortunately, NEO women's wrestling closed its doors for the last time on December 31st, 2010, three weeks before World Wonder Ring Stardom opened theirs. The final NEO era champion, Leon, was defeated by Natsuki Taiyo, now signed to Stardom on 24th July, 2011 to bring the title permanently under Stardom's control. Having been held and contested for by some of the most exhilarating performers to ever appear for Stardom or NEO, the High Speed Championship still lives up to its name and fulfils its promise of guaranteed high octane wrestling whenever it is defended.

1. Natsuki Taiyo

Trained by the legendary Animal Hamaguchi, Natsuki Taiyo was one of the very last wrestlers to debut for the AJW promotion and she did so at the age of 19 on the 3rd of January, 2004. Leaving the company soon after, Taiyo became a wrestler in high demand on the independent circuit, closely associated with the final WWWA Champion Nanae Takahashi, appearing across the broad spectrum of women's promotions for the first two years of her career.

In 2006, Takahashi created the Pro-Wrestling SUN promotion with the backing of ZERO-1 and Taiyo had something resembling a permanent home for the first time. During her tenure with SUN, Taiyo captured the World-1 North American Women's Title, drawing universal praise for her speed and immense technical ability. As SUN folded, Taiyo was once more an independent talent, but one affiliated with Takahashi´s group of ronin wrestlers called Passion Red. The group, consisting of Taiyo, Kana, Ray and Takahashi began appearing in NEO Women's Wrestling and it was here that stablemates Taiyo and Ray contested the first ever match to introduce the High Speed Championship, both wrestlers being the perfect example of lightning fast, hard hitting talents. Taiyo emerged as the first champion and whilst with NEO registered two impressive reigns.

Once NEO closed, Taiyo once again followed Takahashi and she was announced as a day one member of her new promotion Stardom, standing out as one of the most experienced and gifted talents of the fledgling promotion. On the 24th July, 2011, the same day that Takahashi became the first World of Stardom Champion, Taiyo battled the JWP wrestler Leon for the High Speed Championship and, by winning the belt, brought the title under Stardom´s control. This third reign lasted close to two years, during which time Taiyo established herself as a pure blueprint for, not just the High Speed Champion, but for the generation of Stardom talents who would follow in her footsteps.

REIGNS

1. 05/05/2009 (DEFEATED: Ray) - 20/09/2009 (LOST TO: Kaori Yoneyama)
2. 14/03/2010 (DEFEATED: Kaori Yoneyama) - 27/11/2010 (LOST TO: Leon)
3. 24/07/2011 (DEFEATED: Leon) - 02/06/2013 (LOST TO: Kaori Yoneyama)
4. 29/12/2013 (DEFEATED: Kaori Yoneyama) - 06/05/2014 (LOST TO: Io Shirai)

- Combined days as champion: 1,203
- Combined defences: 12

2. Kaori Yoneyama

Kaori Yoneyama began her career with FMW in 1997, moving between numerous promotions in her formative years, including AJW, ARSION and NEO before settling on JWP as her home promotion in the early years of the new millennium.

Her first championship for the promotion was won on July the 6th 2002, the JWP Jr. Championship, through her ability and popularity her reign lasted over two years, after which time she was forced to vacate the championship due to her experience level surpassing that permitted in JWP's junior division. Yoneyama has always worked the broadest spectrum of promotions available to her, well liked by her peers, entertaining as few else can be, combining her technical skills with humour, experience is a factor that would always be in her favour.

On 20th September, 2009, she appeared for NEO Women's wrestling, defeating Natsuki Taiyo for the High Speed Championship, managing only one defence in this first reign due to her commitment as champion to three different promotions simultaneously, Yoneyama lost her title back to Taiyo in March 2010 when she once more appeared for NEO. Still considering JWP her home promotion, she became the JWP Openweight Champion on July 18th, 2010 and on doing so instigated the Yoneyama Revolution, perfectly befitting of her wandering nature, allowing her to defend the title against any wrestler in any promotion. In April of the following year, this rule brought her up against Leon, the reigning High Speed Champion, and a title unification match was fought which Yoneyama lost leading to the JWP Openweight Title being absorbed by the High Speed Championship.

Two more years of Yoneyama's storied career would pass, seeing her travel the world and avoid retirement at the very last moment, before she arrived in Stardom in March 2013 to challenge Natsuki Taiyo once more for the High Speed Championship. This first match ending in a 30-minute draw, it would be their rematch in June that would see Yoneyama regain the Championship which she would hold until the end of the year. No one is wider traveled than Yoneyama, because almost no one is as universally welcomed as her, she continues to be the very freest of freelancers, even welcomed in the guise of Death, as she appeared in summer 2019.

REIGNS

1. 20/09/2009 (DEFEATED: Natsuki Taiyo) - 14/03/2010 (LOST TO: Natsuki Taiyo)
2. 02/06/2013 (DEFEATED: Natsuki Taiyo) - 29/12/2013 (LOST TO: Natsuki Taiyo)
3. 20/07/2019 (DEFEATED: Hazuki) - 10/08/2019 (LOST TO: Riho)

- Combined days as champion: 406
- Combined defences: 3

3. Leon

Wrestling under her real name, Reina Takase made her debut for Hyper Visual Fighting ARSION in March 2000 at the age of 18. It would take her nine months of consecutive losses until she finally picked up a win in her home promotion, proving her resolve by enduring defeat and winning herself great support along the way.

While appearing for AJW alongside her commitment to ARSION, two hugely significant events occurred that would play a major part in her future. On 20th October, 2002, she would team with Kaori Yoneyama for the first time, as both friend and nemesis the chemistry between the two ensuring years of storytelling potential; and on 22nd December, 2002, she became the final ever AJW Jr. Champion, holding the title until the company closed in 2005. With the advent of 2005, AJW having closed and ARSION now renamed AtoZ, Takase went freelance, changing her name to Toujyuki Leon (eventually shortened to just Leon) and adopting her trademark mask.

Appearing for JWP, Leon became Tag Team Champions alongside Kaori Yoneyama on May 15th, going on to hold the titles for a remarkable 15 months, spending the subsequent two years alternatively teaming or feuding with Yoneyama. 2009 saw JWP invaded by Nanae Takahashi´s Passion Red group, a lengthy feud which saw Leon heavily involved in battling the raucous invaders. On 27th of November, 2011, Leon defeated Passion Red member Natsuki Taiyo to become the NEO High Speed Champion, in doing so taking the title to JWP following NEO´s closure.

As part of her lengthy reign, Leon fought Yoneyama once more and in victory unified the NEO High Speed and the JWP Openweight titles before making her one and only appearance for Stardom in defence of the High Speed title on 24th July, 2011. Following her loss to Natsuki Taiyo, Leon returned to JWP and continued at the top of the card, acting as international ambassador for both it and its successor, Pure-J Pro, representing the very best that the company had.

REIGNS
1. 27/11/2010 (DEFEATED: Natsuki Taiyo) - 24/07/2011 (LOST TO: Natsuki Taiyo)
Combined days as champion: 239
Combined defences: 3

4. Io Shirai

Having started appearing for Stardom in its first year of business with an established five year career as a spectacular trailblazer, Io Shirai had some previous history with Natsuki Taiyo whom she had battled in both NEO and ICE Ribbon in tag team contests. Early in her Stardom tenure it was natural for her to revisit this history and the High Speed Championship was her aim when she fought Taiyo on 25th of March, 2012 though she was defeated. As she was when she challenged Taiyo and Yoshiko for the Goddesses of Stardom titles alongside Mayu Iwatani on 20th January, 2013.

All things changed for Shirai a few months later when she captured Stardom's top title, The World of Stardom Championship, and embarked on a record setting reign during which she was utterly unstoppable. At Stardom's third anniversary show, High Speed Champion, Taiyo, challenged for Shirai's title, but was defeated, leading to a return match in May where Shirai challenged Taiyo with Taiyo's belt on the line. In resounding victory, Shirai became a double champion, the first woman to hold the World of Stardom and High Speed Championships at the same time.

In August, Yoshiko took the World of Stardom Championship and in December Io Shirai, as part of Heisei-Gun won the Artist of Stardom title, but had seldom defended the High Speed Championship. Her two defences came against Koguma, a one night tournament winner in her home town, and against former champion Kaori Yoneyama at Stardom's 4th anniversary show. Io lost the belt one month later, in a rematch with newcomer Koguma, giving the young wrestler a hugely significant feather in her cap, before Shirai continued her career at the very top of Stardom's pecking order.

REIGNS
1.   06/05/2014 (DEFEATED: Natsuki Taiyo) - 22/02/2015 (LOST TO: Koguma)
Combined days as champion: 292
Combined defences: 2

5. Koguma

Joining Stardom at the age of fifteen following a public audition, having moved to Tokyo on completing Junior High school with the aim of becoming a pro-wrestler, Koguma debuted on the 4th of November, 2013. Despite an initial run of defeats, a very bright future was expected for the teenager, dubbed the female Kazuchika Okada in press clippings of the time.

After a strong debut year, on November 24th 2014, Koguma won a one night tournament in her home province of Fukuoka to challenge Io Shirai for her High Speed Championship. Despite experiencing defeat, a strong performance and the strong crowd support she received truly seemed to signify a transition from the role of novice to that of a more featured wrestler. In keeping with this, 2015 started with victories and on the 22nd of February she once more challenged Io Shirai for the High Speed Championship, scoring a huge victory and claiming the title in front of a thousand people in the Korakuen Hall, the infamous night on which Yoshiko clashed with Act.

In the upheaval of the months that followed, Koguma became a double champion, as part of the group Candy Crush, adding the Artist of Stardom to her High Speed title in May. However, just a few weeks later she was defeated by luchadora Star Fire to lose the High Speed Championship and promptly disappeared from wrestling completely. Amidst reports of family issues and company rule infractions Koguma did not attend any events after her 17th of May defeat and Stardom was forced to declare the resignation of this great young talent on 15th of September 2015, at the age of just 17.

REIGNS
1. 22/02/2015 (DEFEATED: Io Shirai) - 17/05/2015 (LOST TO: Star Fire)
Combined days as champion: 84
Combined defences: 1

6. Star Fire

Star Fire was trained for the ring by CMLL´s Arturo Berestain and she made her wrestling debut in 2007 at the age of just 15 in Mexico City. Making her name with independent promotions, her biggest break came in late 2009 when she started to appear for CMLL in Arena Mexico on a regular basis.

Leaving CMLL in 2011 to focus on independent wrestling, the next few years saw Star Fire wrestle for the broadest range of Mexican independents and Lucha Fan Fests, including, fatefully, the LEGEND Fan Fest on 17th of May, 2014 where she was booked to battle the touring Io Shirai for the World of Stardom Championship. Although Io retained, Star Fire made a significant impression over the course of the 15-minute match and was invited to Tokyo that August to appear in Stardom´s annual 5 STAR Grand Prix where once more she made a lasting impression, scoring a win over previous High Speed Champion Kaori Yoneyama.

When she returned to Japan the following spring, she did so on the 12th of April, representing the villainous group Oedo Tai; scoring a non-title win over the reigning High Speed Champion Koguma, Star Fire declared her intention to stay in Japan for a long time. One month later, she fought Koguma again, this time with the title on the line and emerged victorious, the first Mexican High Speed Champion. In June she challenged for the Goddesses and Wonder of Stardom Titles, in July she defended her championship against fellow Oedo Tai member Kris Wolf, everything was going perfectly as Star Fire showed the world what she could do on the grand stage of Stardom.

Sadly, in the early stages of her second defence of her High Speed Championship, she suffered a severe knee injury, her opponent, La Rosa Negra, quickly pinning her to hurry the match to a close, taking the title in the process. It would be two years until Star Fire returned to competition in her native Mexico.

REIGNS

1. 17/05/2015 (DEFEATED: Koguma) - 23/09/2015 (LOST TO: La Rosa Negra)

Combined days as champion: 129
Combined defences: 1

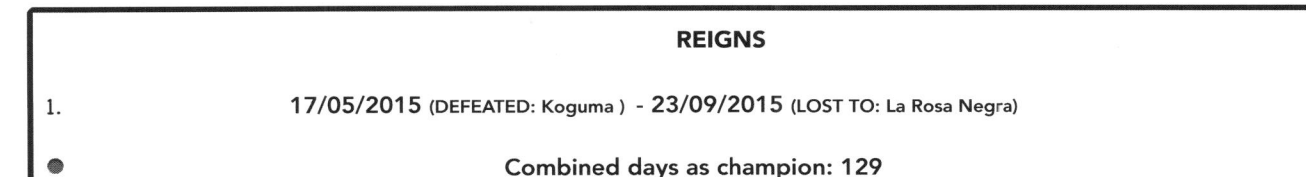

7. La Rosa Negra

Puerto Rican, Nilka García Solís debuted for the World Wrestling Council in 2003 under the name of Black Rose. Becoming WWC Women's Champion three times and having enjoyed a successful run with rival promotion IWA Puerto Rico, the tough technician had achieved all she could on the island and in 2012, under the name La Rosa Negra, began to focus her attention on the mainland U.S. independent scene.

Becoming a champion in Florida and New Jersey, appearing on pay-per-view for SHINE, through 2013 and 2014, La Rosa Negra clashed with the biggest names in American independent wrestling and was able to demonstrate her full range of talents to a broad audience in doing so.

In 2015, following a feud for the NWA World Women's Championship which further enhanced her name value, La Rosa Negra was invited to Japan for the first time, appearing as a member of Oedo Tai and participating in the 5 STAR Grand Prix. 10 days after finishing the tournament with a big win over Mayu Iwatani, La Rosa Negra challenged Star Fire for her High Speed Championship at the Korakuen Hall. Just over two minutes into the match, Star Fire suffered a terrible knee injury and La Rosa Negra took quick advantage to score the victory and become new High Speed Champion.

Two weeks later, in her first defence on 11th of October, La Rosa was defeated by Mayu Iwatani and shortly after returned to the United States. Despite returning to Japan and Stardom in 2017, La Rosa Negra is yet to challenge once more for the High Speed Championship.

REIGNS
1. 23/09/2015 (DEFEATED: Star Fire) - 11/10/2015 (LOST TO: Mayu Iwatani)
Combined days as champion: 18
Combined defences: 0

8. Mayu Iwatani

Two years after her debut, in January 2013, Mayu Iwatani stood alongside Io Shirai to challenge for her first title in the company, The Goddesses of Stardom Championship. Defeated by Natsuki Taiyo and Yoshiko, it would be another six months before Iwatani challenged for her first singles championship, The High Speed Championship, again she was met with defeat, this time at the hands of Kaori Yoneyama.

Having taken 11 months of her career to claim her first win, Iwatani was not short of perseverance and, despite her high speed, high flying style, understood that all things take time and effort. On the final show of 2013, Iwatani claimed her first championship, alongside Hiroyo Matsumoto and Miko Wakizawa she became an Artist of Stardom champion, and the following July she defeated Wakizawa to become a double champion by claiming the Wonder of Stardom Title. Her patience had paid off and at the advent of 2015 Iwatani was considered one of the very top wrestlers in Stardom. She won the 2015 Cinderella Tournament to earn the right to challenge for the World of Stardom title, then she and Io became Goddesses of Stardom in May.

When Iwatani stepped into the ring to challenge La Rosa Negra for the High Speed Championship in October, it would be fair to say the champion was at a disadvantage in terms of momentum and home support. Iwatani emerged triumphant and just a few months later became a triple champion by once more claiming the Artist of Stardom Title.

Although her reign as High Speed Champion was not the longest, she has arguably done much more as champion than anyone else. Through wearing it to the ring in multiple challenges for the World of Stardom title, defending it more than anyone to date in a single reign; by giving a hundred percent to her defences, indeed by giving a hundred percent to everything, Mayu greatly elevates its status and so it was with the High Speed title. Iwatani eventually lost the High Speed Championship after 501 days but within five months was a double World and Wonder of Stardom Champion at the very top of the company.

REIGNS
1. 11/10/2015 (DEFEATED: La Rosa Negra) - 23/02/2017 (LOST TO: Kris Wolf)
• Combined days as champion: 501
• Combined defences: 9

CLASSIC MATCH N°1

Date: 12th March 2016
Location: Shin-Kiba 1st RING, Tokyo
Attendance: 305

MAYU IWATANI vs MOMO WATANABE

The calm before the storm. Mr. Ogawa presenting the title ahead of Mayu Iwatani's blistering 4th defence against one of her greatest long term rivals.

9. Kris Wolf

Kris Hernandez's path into and though wrestling began when, as a freelance photographer working as an English teacher in Japan, she was exposed to World Wonder Ring Stardom via YouTube and fell in love with what she saw. Trained at the Stardom dojo, she made her wrestling debut as Kris Wolf two days before her thirtieth birthday on August 10th, 2014.

Naturally athletic and deeply charismatic, Kris quickly gained respect as a founding member of the Oedo Tai faction, having been one of the final new additions to its predecessor, Kimura Monster-Gun. With a run of victories in summer 2015, Kris earned her first shot at the High Speed Championship, losing to Star Fire on 26th July and going on to spend much of the following year in tag or other multi-person matches.

By the start of 2017, Oedo Tai's fame and the international popularity of Stardom had increased, in no small part due to the charismatic Wolf and her mimetic promos. On 18th of February, Oedo Tai members Kris Wolf and Kagetsu scored a decisive victory over High Speed Champion Mayu Iwatani and Zoe Lucas, which led to a three way match for the championship five days later. Kris defeated Kagetsu and the champion Iwatani to claim the High Speed title. As High Speed Champion, Kris defended her title regularly, successfully four times in five months, falling to Shanna on her fifth defence. In addition to her defences, Kris wrestled in the U.K., Ireland, Spain and debuted for ROH in the USA, working tirelessly as ambassador for the company and her championship.

Just two years later, following a number of concussion related scares, Wolf retired from professional wrestling to hunt down more dreams in pastures new.

REIGNS
1. 23/02/2017 (DEFEATED: Mayu Iwatani) - 16/07/2017 (LOST TO: Shanna)
- Combined days as champion: 143
- Combined defences: 4

10. Shanna

Portugal born Alexandra Barrulas made her pro-wrestling debut in 2006 under the name of Shanna. Over the next seven years she worked hard to gain prominence on the European scene; dedicated to her craft, she won titles in Germany, France and the UK. Always conducting herself with extreme professionalism, Shanna radiated star power which set her apart from her contemporaries and made her greatly in demand across the continent.

An established rival of former World of Stardom Champion, Alpha Female, Shanna also had a long standing in-ring relationship with legend Emi Sakura through her work with the United Kingdom´s Pro-Wrestling Eve. 2013 saw Shanna debut in the USA, winning the International J-Cup with WSU, defeating Nikki Storm in the final. After two more years mixing with the best in the world, she was invited to Stardom in May 2016. As part of a 12 match tour in July, Shanna challenged for the High Speed Championship, earning plaudits in defeat to the all conquering Mayu Iwatani.

Returning to Stardom the following year, as July came around once more, Shanna again challenged for the High Speed Championship, defeating Kris Wolf to win the belt in the Korakuen Hall. In subsequent days she lost two tag-matches involving Mari Apache and in her first defence, just a few weeks later, fell to the legendary Mexican. The following years continuing to bring Shanna the success in Europe that her devotion to the craft deserves.

REIGNS

1. 16/07/2017 (DEFEATED: Kris Wolf) - 13/08/2017 (LOST TO: Mari Apache)

Combined days as champion: 28
Combined defences: 0

11. Mari Apache

Daughter of a man generally regarded to be one of the best trainers of female wrestlers working in Mexico throughout the 80s and 90s, there was a degree of inevitability, to Mariella joining her father's tribe and becoming Mari Apache. Debuting in 1996 for Lucha Libre AAA when she was just 17, her first exposure to Japan came early, cutting her teeth in AJW, Gaea Japan and ARSION in the late 90s.

Her first singles title was won in Japan as she defeated Chaparita ASARI for the Sky High of ARSION Championship in March 2000, eventually losing it to Ayako Hamada in August and returning to focus on her life and career in Mexico.

It would be 2014 before Apache undertook her next tour of Japan, appearing primarily for Pro-Wrestling WAVE from September until the end of the year. It was then in 2017, following the announcement that her daughter Natsumi would begin training to become a pro-wrestler with the Stardom dojo, that Apache first appeared for Stardom. Her second match was a non-title clash with the High Speed Champion Shanna, violent and chaotic, it ended in a double count out; dominant in subsequent tag team clashes involving Shanna, Mari Apache was triumphant when the title was put on the line at the Korakuen Hall on 13th August 2017 to become the High Speed Champion.

As champion, Apache remained in Japan to work a regular schedule for Stardom, her experience and power advantage leading to decisive victories, easily fending off challenges by the likes of Starlight Kid and Saki Kashima. It was at the Year End Climax 2018 show that youth finally overcame experience, Hazuki bringing Apache´s lengthy reign to an end, leading to the legendary warrior returning to Mexico in early 2019.

REIGNS

1. 13/08/2017 (DEFEATED: Shanna) - 24/12/2018 (LOST TO: Hazuki)

- Combined days as champion: 498
- Combined defences: 4

12. Hazuki

After passing public audition, Hazuki joined and debuted for Stardom at the age of 16, displaying natural resilience and wisdom beyond her years, she was winning matches within a month of her first appearance on 6th of July, 2014. It was a year which saw her consistently mix with the top tier of Stardom performers from the very start and end with her declared Rookie of Stardom on December 17th. Her first title match was a rematch of her debut, challenging Koguma unsuccessfully for the High Speed Championship in March, 2015.

Following a period of time away from the ring that stretched from August 2015 to late 2016, Hazuki returned under the name HZK, a member of Queen´s Quest alongside Io Shirai and Momo Watanabe. Elevated by her place in the unit, Queen´s Quest brought HZK her first championship, the Artist of Stardom Title, won on 7th of January 2017; though she was once more unsuccessful when challenging for the High Speed Championship, losing to Kris Wolf in March of the same year. Pride of Stardom, HZK represented the company and Queen´s Quest in one-off appearances for Marvelous and K-Dojo whilst continuing to contend for top titles at home, 2017 ending with a classic clash with Io Shirai over the Wonder of Stardom Championship.

Following the Stardom draft event of April 2018, HZK changed allegiances and became a member of Oedo Tai, with the move she reverted her name to Hazuki and an all together darker change came over her aspect. Clad in black and under the leadership of Kagetsu, the wholesome HZK was replaced by a more compelling, vicious competitor. Unsuccessfully challenging for the Wonder of Stardom and the Women of Honor championships, by the end of the year Hazuki was full of frustration which she unleashed on reigning High Speed Champion, Mari Apache, defeating her to become champion on Christmas Eve 2018. As champion, Hazuki battled to boost the prestige of the title, unafraid to defend it, becoming the first woman to do so in the USA and embodying the best qualities of the women who had gone before her.

REIGNS
1.   24/12/2018 (DEFEATED: Mari Apache) - 20/07/2019 (LOST TO: Death Yama-San)
Combined days as champion: 208
Combined defences: 8

CLASSIC MATCH N° 2

Date: 17th February 2019
Location: Korakuen Hall, Tokyo
Attendance: 820

HAZUKI vs AZM

At only 16 years of age, AZM pushes the veteran Hazuki (20 years old) to the limit before ultimately failing to capture the High Speed Championship. The future of Stardom is bright and moves at the speed of light.

13. Riho

Under the tutelage of Emi Sakura, Riho debuted at the age of 9 in an exhibition contest with Nanae Takahashi, before going on to start a full time schedule at the age of 10 with ICE Ribbon on the 25th of July 2006. Protected in the ring by often working with familiar opponents, frequently her trainer, Riho grew up and developed strength and speed in the public eye.

She captured her first title, the ICE Ribbon Tag Team Championship, alongside Yuki Sato in October 2008 and as Riho proceeded to capture further ICE Ribbon Championships she continued to grow in confidence, becoming the youngest person to ever main-event the Korakuen Hall in May 2010.

In 2012, Emi Sakura established a new promotion, Gatoh Move, a joyous, bespoke wrestling company which Riho joined full time on its first Japanese tour in October. The following year, Sakura and Riho met in a pair of matches for Keiji Mutoh's new WRESTLE-1 promotion, bringing the wrestling prodigy to a wider audience. Capturing the IWA Triple Crown Title from Sakura in November 2014, Riho went on to hold the belt for over a year, putting in one commanding performance after another one whilst beginning to appear for an ever broader range of promotions.

In May 2017 Riho travelled outside of Asia for the first time, appearing alongside Emi Sakura for Pro-Wrestling EVE in a two-night tournament to crown the EVE Champion; she reached the semifinal and the event marked a further step toward international stardom. Following her signing with her former ICE Ribbon and DDT-Pro colleague, Kenny Omega's, new company AEW for shows in the United States, Riho made her debut appearance for Stardom in August 2019, capturing the High Speed Championship in her first match in a three-way also involving Death Yama-san and the Starlight Kid.

Currently performing with two of the biggest wrestling companies in the world with a lifetime's experience behind her, Riho is remarkably still at the very start of her journey and is sure to go on to achieve ever greater things.

REIGNS
1. 10/08/2019 (DEFEATED: Death Yama-san) - 26/07/2020 (LOST TO: AZM)
Combined days as champion: 351
Combined defences: 1

14. AZM

A product of the Stardom Dojo in perhaps the most complete sense, Azumi started her training at the age of nine, making her debut for the company shortly after her 11th birthday against the High Speed archetype and her role model, Natsuki Taiyo. Growing into the full time Stardom schedule by the time she was 15, competing against the strongest and quickest talent in the world forged Azumi into a quick-witted technical wonder. She was spurred on even further by her young rivals Starlight Kid and Hazuki, who forced her to prove herself again and again at the forefront of Stardom's hyper-competitive youth movement.

When she became a member of Stardom's premier stable, Queen's Quest, in early 2017, Azumi became AZM and found herself in a more prominent position on the card; she claimed her first championship, the Artist of Stardom title, as part of the group in April of the same year.

AZM would first challenge for the High Speed Championship when she battled Hazuki in February 2019. This match began a series of unsuccessful challenges for the title which saw her thwarted repeatedly, giving way to an open obsession with claiming the belt. Fixated on the championship, AZM petitioned Stardom to create a High Speed tournament and her pleas were instrumental in the creation of the High Speed Grand Prix in early 2020. However, the pandemic struck and the tournament was called off before its completion, again blocking AZM's destined path to the title.

When Stardom returned from hiatus, Riho's second High Speed title defense put her against both Stardom Kid and AZM on the 26th July 2020; AZM emerged triumphant and with victory claimed the High Speed Championship at only 17 years of age. The championship and her first reign with it is the culmination of AZM's life's work, yet, as she reminds us by stepping straight into 2020's 5 Star Grand Prix, AZM's remarkable life has barely begun and the best is yet to come.

REIGNS

1. 26/07/2020 (DEFEATED: Riho and Starlight Kid) - (CURRENT)

Combined days as champion: 120+
Combined defences: 2+

Acknowledgements

First and foremost forevermore, this book is dedicated to my beautiful daughter Arene-James.

This book would not exist without Nerea, Chris, Aya, Sam Gardiner or Jon Snowden.

This book would not be as good as it is without the friendship and advice of Juel Al-Amin, Erin Garcia Muñoz, Luke Eatwell, Asuka, Yu, Edmond Shields, Miriam Schäfer, Jana Bulloch, Gino Gambino, Joe E Legend, Sydney Jones, Kris Wolf, Sandra and Monica Betolaza, Eddie Edwards, Dan Ball, Sam Fain, Hisame, Sean Radican, Jacob 'IQ Wrestler' Millis, Aidan Kilbride, Mike Connell, Dave Reno, Chris Vice, Hartley Jackson, Ciaràn Hayward, George Delis, Xyon Mckell, AKARI, Will Henderson, Andrew and Stella Papson, Abraham Delgado, Rob McCauley, Michelle Cain, Ane Alonso and Ruben Olveira.

Thank you all so much.

Final notes, obvious stuff, but there's space on the page and these things can't be said enough...Black lives matter, Trans lives matter, the life of every man, woman and child on this earth, regardless of race, gender, religion, sexual orientation or wage bracket matters.
You matter, keep going, keep trying to be kind, keep doing your best, if today isn't your day, tomorrow might be, so keep waking up with good intentions and hope in your heart.
To all writers, artists, dancers, musicians, sculptors, film makers, comedians, poets and professional wrestlers, please remember that you are channeling the divine in pursuit of what you do. You are not merely content creators. Do not willingly accept the label given to you by the corporations and media companies who will profit from your blood, sweat and tears without ever caring for what you do, do not commodify everything you are...we exist to do much more than feed an algorithm and try to trick others into buying our thoughts.

That said.

Thank you for buying this book.

Matt.
25th November, 2020.

Printed in Great Britain
by Amazon